Generis

PUBLISHING

Islamophobia in the United States

Dr. Navid Ghani

Title: Islamophobia in the United States

ISBN: 979-8-88676-045-3

Author: Dr. Navid Ghani

Cover image: https://pixabay.com/

Publisher: Generis Publishing
Online orders: www.generis-publishing.com
Contact email: info@generis-publishing.com

PREFACE

Twenty years have elapsed since America was attacked by Al-Qaida terrorists that shocked the world. Since then the world changed and so did America. With continuing high levels of immigration during the last twenty years, Americans have become increasingly mindful of their cultural diversity mix and its social and political issues. This awareness has heightened the media's negative portrayal of growing Muslim population. Prejudice and bigotry against Muslims persist as obstacles to achieving a society where all individuals and groups feel safe and equal. Today, anti-Islam sentiments continue to be directed at individuals and groups within the Muslim American community.

This book is designed to cover anti-Muslim and anti-Islam sentiments, which are called Islamophobia. It is a highly ambivalent term and while complicated to explain, it is widespread in America and across continents. It is relatively new terminology that was used in Europe in the late 20th century and achieved its horrible peak after the 9/11 terrorist attacks and particularly during the Trump administration.

The accumulation of experiences and perspectives from my daily associations and interactions with American society were the genesis of this study. This study is an attempt to provide a description with greater nuances and an analysis of a complex set of phenomenon, which has been, described alternatively as racist, violent, anti-immigration and Islamophobic.

Unfortunately, one problem was the defamation suffered by many Muslims due to the well-publicized terrorist activities of a small group of radical and extremist thugs. I realized that the general public both in the United States and around the world had focused on these negative occurrences and overlooked the contributions that many Muslims and other immigrants had made and are still making in the benefit of humanity.

When I was married in 1989, my experiences as part of a couple and then a family with anti-Muslim sentiments against immigrants were supported by similar accounts from our Muslim-Norwegian friends who had similar experiences of being "out group" and undesirable in Norwegian society. My subsequent emigration from Norway to the United States in 1995 to attend graduate school added another dimension to the story, and I have included many particulars of my American experience with the same anti-Muslim rhetoric such as "undesirable" and "unwanted" to widen the perspective. American attitudes toward Islam and

Muslims became an especially important subject after Donald Trump was elected president on a right-wing populist platform. Important leaders in the conservative movement embraced aggressive rhetoric about Islam and Muslims. For example, author and columnist Ann Coulter responded to terror attacks by declaring, "We should invade their countries, kill their leaders and convert them to Christianity." Several prominent conservatives have consistently promoted the narrative that the war on terror is part of a larger struggle between Islam and the West, and that an American defeat will set the stage for the Islamic conquest and subjugation of Western countries. People like Michael Flynn, Pat Robertson, Brigitte Gabriel, David Horowitz, Robert Spencer, Daniel Pipes who represent different hate groups and many other conservative activists, including some segments of the social media promote the idea that intolerance and terror are the direct result of Islam's core beliefs and Americans have to fight against the "Islamization" of America.

This study examines the rise of Islamophobia directed against Muslims in contemporary American society. Some basic questions draw my interest in this study: Why do some people carry out acts of violence and hatred against religious minorities and others associated with them? What are the motivations of the perpetrators? And how is their vicious behavior influenced by responses from their social environment including media's coverage of anti-Muslim sentiments defined as Islamophobia?

This study also examines the rise of Islamophobic groups and their hatred towards Muslim and their religion, Islam. We will look at the characteristics of these groups and their members, and try to find out what kinds of events, circumstances and motives these groups might have for attacking Muslims. Recent political discourse under Donald trump presidency further encouraged hate groups to promote Islamophobic acts in the United States. These groups continue to be a well-funded, tight knit network, with some enjoying mainstream political and social clout. Each of the chapters of this book will formulate and explore in greater detail, different aspects of these general issues.

The study applies qualitative methods such as interviews and media reporting of events and incidents on Islamophobic groups and their hatred against Islam.

During this research period a wide range of official, academic and other reliable sources of data were examined, including direct observations of events, media accounts, blogs and creative works, and documents from law enforcement agencies such as the Federal Bureau of Investigation and the United States Department of Justice. Looking at all the sources used in this study, it appears that Western values are associated with the Christian faith and belief system, while Eastern ones are connected to the Muslim faith. The various chapters have been written in a time span of several years, dating back to 2016, to counteract the fear of Islamophobia. I have tried to incorporate the major developments until the end of 2020, but also a few noteworthy events, which took place in 2021 up until the day when the whole manuscript was submitted to the publisher. A close study of relevant events and incidents uncovers a variety of organized and unorganized perpetrators, mixed motives, and different types of responses. No single description can explain the hatred against one religious minority group. Neither can one can explain "Why Islamophobia is becoming widespread and entrenched?' or "why do some people believe in the ideology of hatred and turn violent against others who are different from them?"

I hope this study can serve as a fraction of the knowledge produced on social phenomenon such as Islamophobia. As courtesy demands, I wish to acknowledge the sole responsibility for all the shortcomings, deficiencies and limitations evident in this work.

Dr. Navid Ghani
New York, February 2022

ACKNOWLEDGEMENTS

In recent years since I have conceived the idea of the book, many unexpected incidents have affected its progress. As often happens, it's completing proved far more time-consuming than originally intended. However, I have had the support of many people and organizations along the way. These experiences persuaded me that there has been an unwritten human experience, different from that depicted in official statistics and media reports that needed to be told. I want to thank everyone for their advice and encouragement for the idea and success of this book project. I also want to thank those individuals from various racist groups for having shared their experience with me. I did not mention their name and identity in the study, as they preferred to remain anonymous.

I would like to mention the Carter Center in Atlanta, Georgia for convening an international symposium to develop a strategic response to counter Islamophobia, and the Council on American-Islamic Relations (CAIR) in Washington, D. C., who have been very active in combatting Islamophobia and have a successful track record in its defense of civil liberties and tolerance. The Carter Center was named after president Jimmy Carter, a Nobel's Laureate, who dedicated this center for the purpose of advancing democracy and human rights.

I also wish to thank Anna Rothman, my editor at Generis Publishing Company, who enthusiastically welcomed the idea to bring about this book and for her simply indispensable advice and constant follow-up with the book project. I am happy to have been able to deliver on her kind and timely invitation. Anna has my gratitude for her faith in me and in this project. Last, but not least, I also want to thank to the readers of my prior journal publications of the same study who encourage me to take the arduous path to bring forth a new and expanded description to reflect more recent research. I can only hope that its publication meets, at least in part, their high expectations.

Finally, my gratitude to my family, to my wife Rubina, and my daughters, Maira, Hina, Nimra and my son-in-laws Sheharyar Ali and Zaid Iqbal for their support and encouragement for the success of this project.

To you all, I say stay safe and God bless America!

Dr. Navid Ghani
New York, February 2022

TABLE OF CONTENTS

CHAPTER 1

INTRODUCTION AND BACKGROUND

In 2017, Michael Hari planted a pipe bomb in the Dar Al-Farooq Islamic Center, located in Minneapolis, during morning prayer. Fortunately, there were no casualties, but the attack instilled fear in the Muslim community within the suburban Minneapolis area that was once a safe haven. Upon investigation, prosecutors discovered Hari was the founder of the White Rabbit Militia Group, a White-supremacist militia group with a stockpile of weapons, which they used to terrorize the local Muslim community. The attack on the Dar Al-Farooq Islamic Center is just one example of the Islamophobic sentiment running rampant within the United States. These sentiments fuel hate groups such as the White Rabbit Militia, who use violence and propaganda to terrorize Muslims. This targeted harassment is broadcast and sometimes supported in the media, which negatively impacts the safety, health and social standing of Muslims throughout America.

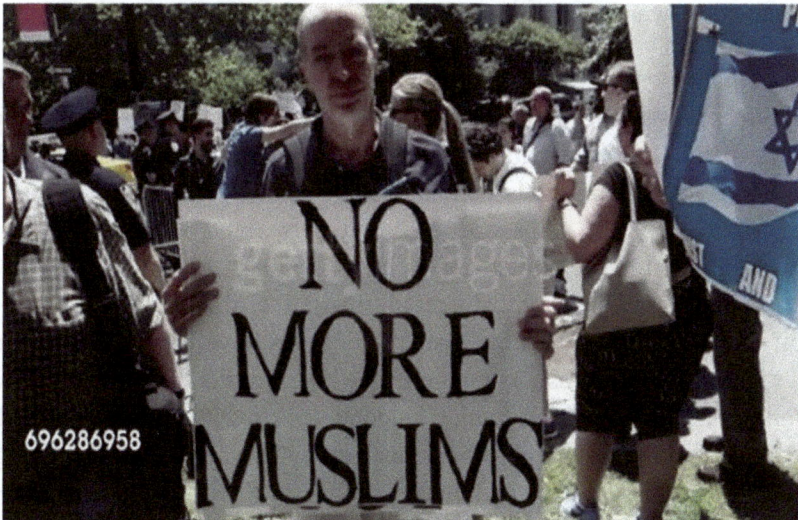

Figure 1: *Anti-Islamophobic rally in New York*
Source: *Reuters*

With the growing number of immigrants and refugees from Muslim countries as well as terrorist attacks committed by Islamic fundamentalists over the last few decades, it is a common argument that antagonism towards Muslims have increased. A new concept has appeared: Islamophobia. It has attracted the attention of academics, social scientists, politicians, and other civil society actors involved. The term "Islamophobia" captures a sentiment that might lead to the discrimination of Muslims, which in turn could lead to hate crimes ranging from verbal insults to physical assault and vandalism. The Council on American Islamic Relations (CAIR), whose mission is to enhance understanding of Islam, has stated that Islamophobia has moved from the edge of American social consciousness to the mainstream of its social and political change (CAIR, 2016). Even more recently, particularly after the 2016 general elections, the media report that Islamophobic hate groups and their activities have tripled since Trump's election campaigns at state and local level. Deadly shootings, torched mosques, vandalized homes and businesses, and young people harassed at school have animated the acutely violent post-election years (Fuchs, 2018). In the United States, the concept of Islamophobia is a widely used in public and scholarly circles today. However, Anti-Semitism, racism, and xenophobic hate crimes are nothing new. During the nineteenth and early twentieth centuries, anti-Semitic sentiments and movements against Jews had strong popular support from the United States. As for Japanese Americans, they were forced to relocate and were incarcerated in camps in the interior of the country after the Pearl Harbor attack in 1941, and Japanese phobia was at its peak.

During the post-war period, especially in the 1960's, public discourse in the United States was strongly anti-racist and moralistic. Racism was considered bad for America and the civil rights movement stood against discrimination and hate crimes based on sex, religious beliefs, and gender. However, things started to change when people of color with different norms and values, especially the Muslims, migrated to the United States in the 1970's and 1980's. The growing numbers of immigrants from Muslim countries and terrorist attacks committed by Muslim fundamentalists over the last few decades have triggered anti-Muslim feelings in the United States. For example, the hostage situation during the Iranian Revolution of 1979, in which Iranian students took over the American embassy and kidnapped dozens of embassy personnel, caused a spike in hate crimes against Muslims in the United States and elsewhere. Despite this event's impact on the Muslim community, the bombing of the Twin Towers by Islamic terrorist group, al-Qaeda, on September 11, 2001 had the most significant and long-lasting impact on many Muslim-Americans.

In the following decades, many more Muslim immigrants and refugees came to the United States as a result of international wars, civil wars or unrest in their home countries. The expanding population of migrants, workers, and refugees emerged as a political and social problem in the United States, reinforcing already growing anti-immigration sentiments. Ekman (2015) argues that social discourse such as "Islam is not compatible with democracy" and that Muslims receive special treatment, such as off from school or job on their religious holidays, clearly indicates an anti-Muslim discourse. Ekman is undoubtedly right about this discourse being principally associated with Muslims; however, this study suggests that the construction of "the Muslim" identity is mainly built around images of Muslim culture and the religion of Islam.

Polarization of American Society

Polarization of American society can be easily observed in media reporting, as we have seen in recent years. The U.S. social media are increasingly critically engaged in this endeavor with their contribution in spreading negative stereotypes of Muslims and other minority groups. Anti-Muslim hate crimes often have distinctive features that differentiate them from other types of hate crimes. These hate crimes target people or property associated, or perceived to be associated, with Muslims such as mosques, religious and community centers, Muslim families' homes, Muslim cemeteries, and schools. There are also numerous incidents in which, for example, women wearing headscarves are the victims of assault. Such anti-Muslim hate crimes take place across the United States and their prevalence has increased significantly in recent years, easily surpassing the peak reached in 2001, the year of the September 11th terrorist attacks.

According to the Pew research Center, in 2016, there were 127 reported victims of aggravated or simple assault, compared with 91 the year before and 93 in 2001. These attacks have ranged from trashing mosques, to death treats, to arson and vandalism. However, a very limited number of these attacks have been covered in American mainstream media. Attacks where the perpetrator is Muslim, on average, are covered twice as often as those committed by non-Muslims or where the victims are Muslims (Katayoun, 2017). This alarming statistic shows that there is discrepancy between the roles that media takes when it comes to different types of hate crimes. The most common explanation for this bias centers on the perceived link between Muslims and terrorism, as well as the role of media in reinforcing this association in public perception. Ample studies have revealed that Muslims are frequently associated with extremism and terrorism in various media outlets, and that these media portrayals influence public opinion of both Muslims and Islam as their religion. For example, Panagopoulos (2006) and Ciftici (2012) argued that members of most Western societies are becoming

15

increasingly anxious about Islam's compatibility with the "Western" values of tolerance, acceptance and civility, and individuals who believe that Muslims remain culturally distinct are more likely to have negative attitudes about them. Unfortunately, it is not just American Muslims who are impacted by Islamophobia (fear or hatred of Islam). It is the American society at large that, by virtue of prejudice against Islam and Muslims, comes to imbibe a display of lies and distortions, which is contrary to American creed of equality and justice and is thus detrimental to social harmony and social inclusion. In addition to fueling hatred for Muslims, Islamophobia in the media can seriously impact the well-being of Muslims in the United States. It can make peaceful and law-abiding people feel unwelcomed in a place that is meant to be their home. Many Muslims may also be reluctant to speak up about the effects of Islamophobia on them and their families, and this is worrying, as staying silent and not reporting Islamophobic incidents to authorities can further exacerbate an already difficult situation.

Americans started to discover more about Muslims and Islam through events that had an international impact, such as the 9/11 attacks, subsequent terrorist attacks in Madrid and London, the Danish cartoons crisis, and attacks in Brussels, Paris and St. Bernardino in California and so forth. These incidents became discursive events that shaped the debates on Islam in the United States and elsewhere. Through these developments the passive image of Muslims transformed into one that was aggressive and violent. The waves of violent acts in recent years specifically at Muslims have caused fear and concern in the United States. Particularly in the election campaign of 2016, President Donald Trump had frequently played on Islamophobia to increase his popularity. He is the most visible American businessman-turned-politician to capitalize on anti-Muslim sentiment. His call for open profiling and surveillance of Muslims, the Muslim ban from certain Muslim countries – a process that is largely already underway – and claim that "Islamic terrorism" is a biggest threat to the Untied States can certainly fuel hate-oriented Islamophobia.

Moreover, migration is nowadays facilitated by improved transport, communications, and substantial immigrant communities in the United States. Public opinion is worried about continuing immigration both from Muslim countries and non-Muslim countries and in this climate, it is easy for racist or xenophobic individuals and groups to gain support and strength. Unfortunately, hate has become a key factor in American society and, due to today's political and social discourse, the anti-Islam and anti-Muslim Muslim sentiments in America have become more prominent. It is detrimental to our constitutional foundation that is focused on equality, liberty, and freedom of expression.

Today, "Islamophobia" is the most widely recognized and employed term to label the various manifestations of anti-Muslim experiences and prejudices, such as negative attitudes, discourses and practices against Muslims and Islam by the media, politicians and members of the non-Muslim communities. But what is Islamophobia, exactly?

In what follows, is defining Islamophoia, a conceptual discussion, theoretical and methodology approaches and some of the limitations of the data. In addition, much of the literature will, however, be discussed in connection with the various chapters wherever it is relevant to the topic concern.

CHAPTER 2

THEORETICAL AND METHODOGICAL APPROACHES

Islamophobia defined

It is important to conceptualize and define terms early on so that the readers can have a full understanding of the overall analysis and the arguments being made. The following terms are briefly defined to provide context and an understanding for the discussion on the main term "Islamophobia" used in this study:

Islam	**the religious faith of Muslims including belief in God (Allah) as the sole deity and Muhammad as his prophet.**
Muslim	a follower of the religion of Islam.
Radical Islam or Islamism	a set of extreme and violent beliefs resulting from a distortion of the mainstream religion, Islam. Radical Islam and Islam are regarded as two different entities, which are not to be confused with each other.

Researchers and social scientists define Islamophobia as an exaggerated fear, hatred, and hostility toward Islam and Muslims that is perpetuated by negative stereotypes resulting in bias, discrimination, and the marginalization of Muslims (Bleich, 2011). This concept has become a real danger to the foundations of democratic order of the United States. Furthermore, it has also become the main challenge to the social peace and coexistence of different cultures, religions and ethnicities within the country. As a social discourse, Islamophobia is in its infancy and has largely sprung due to the negative attitudes and hatred that have emerged in the post 9/11 contexts, which saw the conflation of Muslims, being considered a threat to western economy and civilization. Although its prevalence is difficult to measure, Islamophobia seems most widespread in the United States, as well as to varying degrees in other countries.

A conceptual discussion: Islam Vs. West

The term "Islamophobia" has become well known in academia as much as in the public discourse. Islamophobia operates by creating static 'Muslim' identity, which is attributed in negative terms and generalized for all Muslims. Erik Bleich (2011) describes it as harmful rhetoric and actions directed at Islam and Muslims in Western democracies. According to Bleich, the term not only identifies anti-Islamic and anti-Muslim sentiments, it also provides a language for denouncing them. Similarly, according to Zuquete (2008), Islamophobia is "a widespread mindset and fear-laden discourse in which people make blanket judgments of Islam as the enemy of the west." Thus, Islamophobia is simply another reincarnation of this unfortunate trend of bigotry, resulting in prejudice on the one hand and hatred on the other. According to the British historian Norman Daniel, little has changed since the eleventh century: "The earliest Christian reactions to Islam were something like those of much more recent date. The tradition has been continuous and alive" (Allen, 1980). The term "Islamophobia", he argued, was coined to define this age-old, though growing, hostility against Islam and Muslims. Indeed, as seen in the United States, Islamophobia denotes a range of negative feelings towards Muslims and their religion, Islam, which can manifest in the form of hate crimes, physical and verbal assault, vandalism on mosques, and defamation of Islam in the media. Widely debated even before the 9/11 attacks, this concept of the "Clash of Civilizations" or "Islam vs. West" is based on the premises that there are fundamental differences between Islam and the West, and on the idea that Muslims might be undermining society from within. This notion fueled hostility on the assumption that Muslim culture is incompatible with liberal, democratic and secular American values, and that Muslims therefore do not belong in America. Such rhetoric, however, cannot justify the underlying reasons for anti-Muslim prejudice on the part of mainstream America or elsewhere. Although its prevalence is difficult to measure, the reality is that Islamophobia seems to be most widespread within the American social, political and institutional mechanisms, which produce such hostility towards Muslims and Islam.

In short, and particularly during and the aftermath of November 2016 presidential election, the term Islamophobia has quickly come into general use throughout the United States in political and social discourse and thus made life difficult for American Muslims. Donald Trump in one of his tweets called for a total and complete shutdown of Muslims entering the United States. Trump followed his proposal with an email to reporters in December 2015, "Without looking at the various polling data, it is obvious to anybody the hatred is beyond comprehension. Where this hatred comes from and why we will have to determine. Until we are able to determine and understand this problem and the dangerous threat it poses, our country cannot be the victim of horrendous attacks by people that believe only in Jihad, and have no sense of reason or respect for human life" (Blumberg, 2017). By this statement Trump did not distinguish between extreme groups of violent fanatics and the rest of the world's nearly 1.8 billion Muslims.

Theoretical approach

This section will discuss theoretical approaches, typologies, the nature of the phenomenon, and some of the literature in the field. The act of violence strongly connotes with behavior that is in some sense considered illegitimate and unacceptable in society. Some perpetrators see their act of violence in the context of political ideology within which their violent acts appear not only acceptable but also even admirable. Such ideology or discourse is typically at odds with the mainstream values in which they live. Later chapters will describe in detail how anti-immigration activists both politicians' and social actors and right-wing extreme groups and organizations have strikingly similar ideologies which legitimize violence and hate crime against immigrants and minorities. In short, these discourses describe how this is played out in the context of anti-Muslim sentiment. Below are a few examples of these accounts:

A man participating in a white supremacist rally drove a car into a crowd in Charlottesville, Virginia in August 2017, which resulted in a casualty. President Trump insisted that he needed to know the facts before making a statement. A few hours later, an Uzbek immigrant inspired by the self-described Islamic State killed eight people by plowing his truck down a bike path in lower Manhattan in October 2017. Right after this incident, Trump was active social media and tweeted about ISIS and placing heavier restrictions on the country's immigration system.

In a November 2017 segment on "The Daily Show," host Trevor Noah summed it up by saying: "When it was a Nazi, then Trump needed more facts. When it was a Muslim, that was the only fact that he needed."

Although several explanations may be pertinent to hate crime incidents or violence and the way it plays out, no existing criminological theory can fully account for the transformation from prejudice to violent or criminal behavior by perpetrators. Perhaps the most common theory that has been used to explain hate crime – at least in part – is the typologies of hate perpetrators developed by

Mcdevitt and Bennett (2002). To explain hate crimes using typology research, they argue that the interplay of several different factors, such as social, psychological, and contextual, must be considered, as these contribute to hate crimes and violence Additionally, other important factors for consideration include perpetrators' motives, victims' characteristics, and cultural ideologies about the victims' social groups. According to this typology, these perpetrators of hate crime are characterized as thrill-seeking individuals and groups who act in response to other hate crimes. In other words, they commit hate crimes to protect their neighborhood from perceived outsiders, and are strongly committed to bigotry, so they turn hatred into a pattern. According to this theory, most thrill-seeking crimes are assaults on individuals who are vulnerable or easy targets that cannot or will not fight back. Hate groups can often be compared to gangs who have a territory they need to protect and make sure other people they don't agree with infiltrating their area. Various other researchers have concurred with Mcdevitt and Bennett's findings that perpetrators frequently seek out the excitement of a hate attack (Byers, Crider, & Biggers, G. K., 1999). Their findings suggest that a large proportion of hate crimes committed by young men will be motivated, at least partly by an immature urge to seek thrills and excitement. The Dar-Al-Farooq Islamic Center bombing mentioned earlier is an example of perpetrators who, after the bombing attack, recounted that in addition to scaring immigrants they wanted media attention and publicity that would make people realize that at least someone is doing something for the good of the society.

According to a 2017 CNN report, the most prominent reason that people commit a way to seek a thrill is the mission offenders, who commit hate crimes out of a feeling that they are unimportant to the system, so they feel their actions are justified (Burke and Hernandez 2017). The sickening part of these crimes is that perpetrators actually believe that what they're doing is for the best of the society. A good example of a thrill-seeking crime is when an individual or a group attack innocent people or burn religious centers or their grocery stores. In April 2021, a federal grand jury indicted two Los Angeles-area men for conspiracy and hate crime offenses. They attacked five victims of a family-owned Turkish restaurant and threatened to kill them if they would not leave the country. On the day of the attack, one defendant sent a text message saying he planned to go "hunting for Turks." The two men allegedly attacked the restaurant while shouting anti-Muslim slurs, hurling chairs at victims, and cursing them for invading their country. Multiple victims were injured during the attack and there was over $20,000 worth of damage done to the restaurant (USDJ, 2021).

The message being sent to the victims is that they are not welcome here, which results in the victims fleeing from the area, scared of what will happen if they decide to stay. In many cases, the main objective is to gain attention, and the perpetrators are thrilled when the newspapers and other media write stories about them. According to Barbara Perry, one of the most common background characteristics for individuals that join a hate group is that they faced some kind of family disruption in their life. This disruption can range from divorce or parental abandonment to a parent being incarcerated or the individual being abused by their parents. These people are the ones who are attracted to hate groups. Nealeys further argues there's a common misconception that only people from lower economic backgrounds are attracted to these types of groups. This is just not the case, he claims, as people from a wide cross-section of socioeconomic backgrounds become involved as these types of groups have a much wider recruitment potential than are often recognized (Nealey, 2014).

For the more organized racial groups or people, media attention has been a focal object for carrying out violence and hate attacks against innocent people. This has been a continual feature since September 11, 2001, and the goal of such actions is to arouse public opinion and to get an issue on the political agenda. Violent incidents associated with certain groups or individuals who want to seek pleasure and excitement will always be good material for the media because of their newsworthiness. When the 9/11 terrorists flew planes into the World Trade Center in New York City, the Pentagon in Washington, D.C., and a field in Pennsylvania, several thousand innocent people were killed and injured. In addition to scaring Americans, one of the main motives of these terrorists was publicity and media attention about the "atrocities" the United States was involved in, particularly in the Middle East, while supporting Israel. Though Islamophobia was not a common phenomenon at the time, political and social reactions to 9/11 attacks fueled ignorance and bigotry and violence towards Muslims and their religion Islam.

In forming a more comprehensive picture of the types of hate perpetrators, Barbara Perry (2001) argued in her structured action theory that such crimes are better understood as the extreme example form of discrimination, which follows from a culture of discrimination and marginalization of people who are somehow "different". Those who are deemed to be different are resisted because they are feared. Structured action theory explores the relationship between structure and action and among gender, race, and class, and that to understand crime, we must appreciate how crime operates through a complex series of gender, race, and class practices. Crime must be examined by focusing on people in specific social settings, what they do to construct social relations and social structures, and how these social structures constrain and channel behavior in specific ways.

According to Perry, regardless of race, gender or social class, hate perpetrators can be common individuals, neighbors, public employees, and national political representatives whose consciousness and ideology is not very articulated but have played a significant role in intimidating immigrants and marginalized people. Such people are fearful of difference and incite hatred or use rhetoric to discriminate against others. The hate crimes against vulnerable groups are used as examples of how an environment of intolerance is shaped by such negative rhetoric. Powerful words such as "Islamic terrorism" and the "immigrant threat" are provided as illustrations of how perpetrators are given permission to hate others. *These are all ways that Islamophobic hate groups have gained momentum and membership. Arguably the most predominant characteristic of hate groups is fear. Their members may feel that their livelihood or way of life is threatened by demographic changes. Offenders may not be motivated by hate, but rather by fear, ignorance or anger. This means that people are afraid of change and will therefore go to extreme lengths, such as joining and participating in a hate group, to keep their life the way it is. Fear of differences is what drives hate groups. Fear is also vital to hate groups because that is often what they want to incite. Those who are deemed to be different are resisted because they are feared.* Perry argues that those who are deemed to be different are resisted because they are feared. In her structured action theory, she explores the relationship between structure and action and among gender, race, and class, and that to understand crime, we must appreciate how crime operates through a complex series of gender, race, and class practices. Crime must be examined by focusing on people in specific social settings, what they do to construct social relations and social structures, and how these social structures constrain and channel behavior in specific ways.

Perry argues that hate crimes are not an abnormality of current society, but rather a by-product of a society still coping with inequality, difference, fear, and hate. The various forms of discrimination endured by marginalized groups, a product of what Perry terms 'doing difference', can be taken a step further to include more severe acts of prejudice, such as hate violence. Perry uses the phrase 'doing difference' to characterize the way human behavior is shaped and subordination is maintained within the social structures of power and culture. She uses this theory to account for hate crimes and provide an understanding for the ways we can "do difference differently". Proactive strategies can refer to bridge-building efforts and justice through criminal justice system and action against bigotry and violence. She focuses on strategies for social inclusion and restructuring laws to protect the rights of vulnerable and marginalized groups.

Perry argues that various minority groups become the scapegoats for the woes felt by dominant members of society. A good example of this is 9/11, which caused a huge increase in anti-Muslim hate groups seeking revenge for what the terrorists did to the United States. The sad truth is that many people who are victims of these hate groups are peace-loving and against any kind of terrorism. Muslims are still being attacked because they have the same religion or they look the same. They are fearful for their and their children's lives.

From both Mcdevitt and Bennett's conception of 'hate perpetrators' and Perry's use of the term 'doing difference,' we can begin to see violence committed against Muslims and other immigrants as possibly rooted to the perceived bigotry and hatred in a perpetrator's own life, which he or she believes is the fault of such groups. As a result, various minority groups become the scapegoats for the woes felt by dominant members of society. Blaming others for frustration relating to crime and terrorism is amplified, with certain media outlets portraying Muslim and other immigrants as the root cause of society's problem (see chapter "the Role of Media and Islamophobia"). We looked at data from the Federal Bureau of Investigation (FBI) on hate crimes against Muslims and found that this fear is not entirely groundless. According to the FBI, hate crimes against Muslims surged immediately following the terror attacks of 9/11. There were 481 crimes reported against Muslims in 2001, up from 28 the year before (Levin, 2018). The number dropped in the following years, but has never returned to levels reported before the 9/11 attacks (see figure below). In recent years however, annual hate crimes against Muslims have consistently soared in the 100-150 range, roughly five times higher than the pre-9/11 rate (FBI, 2016).

You can see an overall downward trend for hate crimes against other religions in the figure below. But, if you factor out other religions, you'll see hate crimes against Muslims did not follow the general downward trend.

The phenomenon of Islamophobia is still recent and will not disappear any time soon. Future research will need to develop clear theoretical models to account for the causation of hate crimes endured by ethnic and religious minorities.

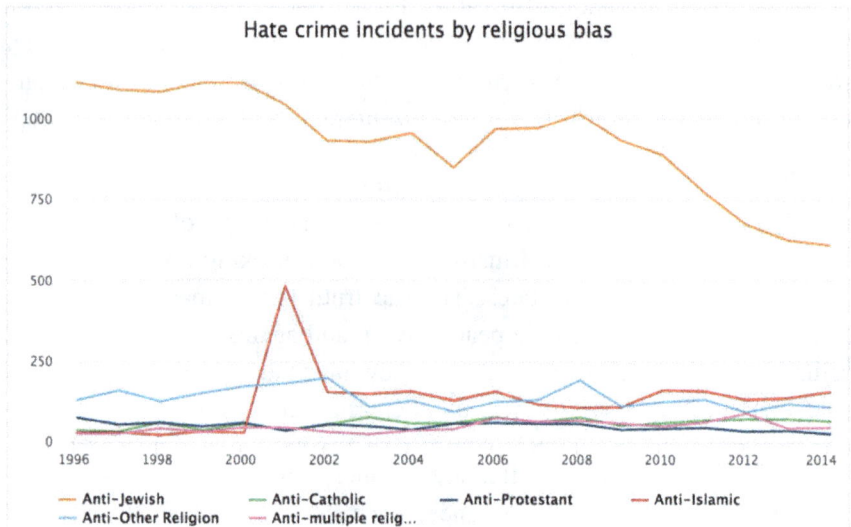

Figure 2: *Hate crime incidents by religious bias*
Source: *FBI. The latest data is for 2014*

In the following, we will discuss the methodological approach for this study and the limitations it had while collecting the data from different agencies.

Methodology

This study applies mainly qualitative methods and some simple data, supplemented by some relevant statistics on hate crimes and acts of violence, types of groups and organizations, types of discourse, types of political and social responses. Yin (1989) proposes two principles for data collection that may increase the reliability and validity of the study. The first principle is the use of multiple sources. Results based on multiple sources are more convincing and provide an opportunity to study the same phenomenon from various angles. This increases the construct validity of the study. My study is therefore based on various sources as discussed below. Yin's second principle of data collection is to maintain a chain of evidence. The reader should be able to follow the writer's logic from the initial theme discussed to the final conclusions. These principles establish the validity and reliability of the study under discussion.

Data for this study are based on a variety of sources, which are as follows:

a) *Direct observation of events*, such as demonstrations and rallies in local communities arranged by local community organizations. Examples of

26

these observations are my participation in the public demonstration on February 19, 2017 in New York in a rally called "Today, I Am a Muslim Too". I also participated in the January 29, 2017 public protest at Battery Park in New York against the executive orders passed by Trump on January 28 to ban Muslim and Muslim refugees from coming to the United States. In both these events, I was a participant as well as an observer. I also observed the right wing extremists marches in New York and Washington, DC, as well as a number of demonstrations and violent clashes between opponent groups. I was also able to interviewed few people who were in these demonstrations. Given the 'religious' nature of Islam and the Islamophobia, no other research method, whether qualitative or quantitative in nature, would have proven more useful and applicable other than participant observation. This is very important because, through participant observation, a better understanding of a social world is made possible. This in turn helps advance our collective knowledge of social phenomena, improve social interaction, and enhance human social life.

b) *Literature review and publications,* based on my own review of extensive material on hate crime and religious violence, and review of international research into the relationship between the media and terrorism, I underscored some of the aspects of Islamophobia in the United States. Also through my own publications on the phenomenon, I have underscored the significance of "Islamophobia" that is widely recognized to label the various manifestations of anti-Muslim experiences and prejudices, such as negative attitudes, discourses and practices against Muslims and Islam by the media, politicians and members of the non-Muslim communities. I also have long had a close collaboration with a local Muslim chaplain and community leader, Nayyer Imam, and a Muslim Deputy District Attorney in New York, Sheharyar Ali, who provided me with highly relevant literature on Islam and the Muslims.

c) *Media accounts* are an important secondary source on incidents and information about Islamophobia. Media accounts can take the form of observing the content and information produced online and other social media and uncovering trends and insights that emerge from this data. Readers should be cautious about media reports because such reports sometimes give incorrect information, and tend to exaggerate events. Media coverage of Islamophobia is therefore also an object of this book and is discussed in chapter on *The Role of the Media.*

d) *Interviews* with persons who have some knowledge of hate crimes based on religious beliefs were conducted in 2020. Most interviews were face-to-face encounters, some were conducted by telephone and some were in the form of brief informal arranged talks. These interviews were unstructured and are good for sensitive topics because they are more likely to make respondents feel at ease with the interviewer. As there are only few interviews, the material therefore does not provide a basis for deeper analysis of the interviewee's arguments. I also had difficulty in getting across to some extreme individuals and groups because of the nature of phenomenon under study and also for my own safety.

e) *Surveys* published by non-profit organizations and activists, such as Council on Islamic American Relations (CAIR), Southern Poverty Law Center (SPLC), and Pew Research Center were very useful in understanding data about violence and perpetrators as well as political, social, and legal responses to such act.

f) *Documents* from the law enforcement agencies such as Federal Bureau of Investigation (FBI) and the Bureau of Justice Statistics (BJS), a federal government agency belonging to the U. S. Department of Justice and a principal agency of the U.S. Federal Statistical System, provide useful information as well. Hate crimes such as threatening ethnic minorities and their places of worships can have a devastating impact upon the communities where they occur, which is one of the reasons why the investigation of hate crimes that fall under federal jurisdiction. The FBI gathers and publishes hate crime statistics from law enforcement agencies across the country. The Bureau's latest hate crime report was released in 2016 and includes information detailing the offenses, victims, offenders, and locations of hate crimes. The 2016 collection marks the 25th anniversary of the Bureau's work in compiling data related to bias-motivated crimes, which began in 1990. Both these agencies publish data regarding statistics gathered from the roughly fifty thousand agencies from all states that comprise the justice system.

Limitations of data

Statistics and reports from these agencies provide useful data about violence and perpetrators as well as legal and political underreporting responses to crime related to racism and Islamophobia. Consequently, the data available is somewhat limited; one of the reasons is that the local police likely provide numbers voluntarily to the FBI who then compiles the statistics for the whole country. A lot of the reporting issues and discrepancies rest on the shoulders of police departments, which share local data with the FBI's Uniform Crime Reporting program. It's at that junction that the statistics representing cases of hate crimes get diluted or tempered. A general perception is that the police departments are far more reluctant to classify certain crimes as hate crimes, fearing that it would paint the community as hateful, or as harboring hateful people. Those concerns still exist today, in spite of the fact that hate crimes have a "severe and profound impact" on the affected communities, in particular communities of color and immigrant communities. There's been a push by the Federal Bureau of Investigation (FBI) to raise awareness about the need to report hate crimes and support victims in recent month. For example, the Atlanta-area spas shootings involved the deaths of six Asian women who owned the spa centers. The man who killed these innocent Asian victims told the police that he saw their businesses as a temptation, which he needed to eliminate. These killings generated an outpouring of solidarity for the Asian community and a movement against anti-Asian racism around the country. Such support reflects the deep trauma associated with hate crimes. Police departments have also come under increased scrutiny in the wake of the death of George Floyd, who was killed after a former Minneapolis police officer knelt on his neck for over nine minutes. Floyd's death was not ruled a hate crime—Minnesota Attorney General Keith Ellison argued that_ "systemic racism, not individual racist motivation was to blame—but it did spark global protests and calls for police reform that highlighted issues of police bias and systemic racism in departments across the U.S.

The level of underreporting of racist hate crimes is closely related to the affected minority's perception of the police. If they deem the police to be biased, victims are unlikely to report their complaints to the police. Interestingly, a study by Bureau of Justice Statistics reveals a far greater number of hate crimes than what is reported. For example, in 2012, an estimated 60 percent of hate crimes were not reported to police (BJS, 2014). The fact that most victims do not report racist-motivated hate crimes because they don't feel it is important or that police would help. Also, many victims do not report their experiences to law enforcement for fear of persecution or reprisal. This shows the limits of hate crime reporting, therefore producing a lack of solid and reliable data on the problem nationwide.

CHAPTER 3

ISLAM AND MUSLIMS IN THE UNITED STATES

Despite being an extremely diverse country, with Muslims being the fastest-growing religious group, the United States has nevertheless been influenced by the post 9/11 hysteria and the recent terrorist attacks mentioned earlier in the book. Many surveys done in recent years suggest that majority of Americans think the Islamic religion is associated with violence and religious extremism. Along with these negative views, which have spurred a general fear of Muslims, majority of Americans admit they know very little about the Islamic religion. Despite Muslims making up a rather sizable selection in the United States, the average person is not likely to understand what it means to be Muslim. In turn, if we are going to look into the hate against Muslims, we must understand the root of this problem. The term Muslim roughly translates to "one who willfully submits to God." In other words, Muslims willingly practical this religion known as Islam. They worship a god, which they refer to as "Allah" and see this holy figure as the creator of all of which we know on this Earth and the universe. Their book of worship is referred to as "The Qur'an" which is also referred to as "The Reading" or "The Recitation." It is made of 114 "Surahs" or chapters. This book, in the Islamic faith, was gifted to Muhammad, the last of Allah's prophets. As Holy Scripture, this book is a collection of Allah's messages to humanity. Muslims follow this scripture as it contains verses on how they should scripture when they pray and worship Allah. Going into Muslim beliefs specifically, the Islamic religion encompasses the "Five Pillars of Faith" and "Six Articles of Faith." The pillars begin as such, Shahadah (The confession of faith), Salat (Prayer), Sawm Ramadan (Fasting), Zakat (Alms Giving), and Hajj (Pilgrimage to Kaaba, Mecca, where the shrine to Islam resides). The six articles are as follows: Monotheism (The main message of Islam is monotheism), belief in the angels, belief in prophets, belief in holy books, belief in Judgment Day, and belief in predestination (belief that Allah knows what will happen to Muslims from the very beginning from every decision from birth until death). The Islamic religion seems standard in terms of religion containing a holy book, a holy being of worship, and varying beliefs and rituals. Muslims are people who practice Islam, a monotheistic religion that promotes devotion and worship of "Allah". Muslims believe in one God, Holy Quran and Prophet Muhammad. The practice of Islam originated in Mecca and Medina of Saudi Arabia during the early 7th century AD. Around this time, Muhammad began to share messages from the Angel Gabriel, who had been sent by God. Muhammad preached and spread the message from God with people in and around Mecca. He gained a large following, and some of his followers wrote down the revelations in what today is known as the Quran. Islam is the predominant religion in certain parts of the world more than others. These countries include: North Africa, the Middle East and South as well as South East Asian countries, though people outside of these regions are also followers of Islam. Many of Islam's followers from these regions speak Arabic. It is similar to Judaism and Christianity in the fact that they have many respected prophets such as Muhammad, Abraham, Moses, Noah, and Jesus. However, in Islam, Muhammad is recognized as the final and most significant prophet. His followers read the Quran, commune for worship at mosques, and abide by Islamic teachings.

Currently, 1.8 billion people practice Islam globally and its global reach has impacted the culture and politics of the United States and European countries. Within the U.S., Islam is associated with mass immigration from Arabic and Middle Eastern countries such as Iraq, Iran, Afghanistan, Saudi Arabia, Egypt, India, Pakistan, and Bangladesh. Mass immigration from these countries increased dramatically after President Lyndon B. Johnson signed the Immigration and Nationality Act of 1965 into law. The act expanded immigration opportunities from countries with significant Muslim populations. Immigration to the United States post-1965 favored those deemed to have specialized educational and skills, thus impacting the socio-economic makeup of American Muslims. The United States began seeing Muslim immigrants arrive in the early 21st century as refugees due to such reasons as political unrest, war, and famine. While the United States has historically led the world in refugee resettlement numbers, admissions fell dramatically under President Donald Trump. In 2020, the United States admitted fewer than 12,000 refugees, much less from the 70,000 to 80,000 admitted annually just a few years earlier and the 207,000 welcomed in 1980, the year the formal U.S. resettlement program began. In 1921, the Biden administration significantly increased the number of refugees admitted to the United States from the historically low 15,000 set by the Trump administration to 62,500. Biden also pledged to admit 125,000 refugees in 2022. However, the slow pace of resettlement procedure in the COVID-19 era made it unlikely that the full number of slots will be filled, at least in 2022. In addition, the growth and regional migration of Muslims – combined with the ongoing impact of the Islamic State in Iraq and Syria (ISIS) and other extremist groups that commit acts of violence in the name of Islam – have brought Muslims and the Islamic faith to the forefront of the political debate in the United States. Anti-Islamic forces always target Muslims and their religion Islam. For instance, anti-Muslim hate crime incidents spiked after September 11th, 2001, jumping from few incidents in 2000 to several hundreds in 2001. These incidents have ranged from hate mail to verbal assaults to crimes that have resulted in deaths. The targets were not limited to people of Middle Eastern descent. It began with the murder of Balbir Singh Sodhi, a 49-year-old Sikh, discussed below under section *"Islamophobic incidents and developments in the United States,"* who was hit outside his gas station in Arizona.

Muslim population in the United States

Before examining the negative public perceptions of Muslims, appropriate context must be provided. Muslims are followers of the religion Islam. The Arabic word Islam means "surrender", specifically, to the will of the one God, called Allah in Arabic. Islam is strictly a monotheistic religion, and its adherents are called Muslims who regard the Prophet Muhammad as that last messenger of God. The American Muslim community represents an enormous diversity of language, culture, and socioeconomic status along with a diversity of Islamic practices. But despite having a presence in the country as far back as the 17th century, Muslims are still often treated as "the other." Muslims face increased scrutiny and backlash on issues ranging from mosques and sharia law to questions of terrorism. Muslim Americans aren't the first religious or ethnic group considered a threat to America's religious and cultural landscape. At the turn of the 20th century, Jewish and Eastern European immigrants were criticized in the mainstream as racially inferior to other Americans. Of course, today those same fears have been projected onto Muslim and other immigrants. The Muslim American case shares with these other immigrant experiences the fact that with a religion different from the mainstream comes the fear that it will dilute, possibly even disrupt, America's thriving religious landscape. Recent political debates in the U.S. over Muslim immigration and related issues such as refugee crisis have prompted many to ask how many Muslims actually live in the country. Answering such a question is not easy, in part because the U.S. Census Bureau does not ask questions regarding religion; therefore, there is no official government count of the U.S. Muslim population. The estimated number of Muslims in the United States varies, depending on the sources. The U.S. Census estimates there are 3 to 6 million Muslims living in the country n 2015. At the highest estimates, the percentage of Muslims in the United States would represent approximately 1 to 2 percent of the population (U.S. Census, 2016). Pew Research Center (PEW) believes the figure is closer to 3.45 million in 2017, including 2.5 million adults and 1.35 million children, making up roughly 1.1% of the total U.S. population; this statistic reveals an increase of 0.7 percent since 2007, due largely to immigration (PEW, 2018). Pew Research Center is a nonpartisan fact tank in Washington D.C. that informs the public about social and political issues (see figure 3 and 4).

Number of Muslims in the U.S. continues to grow

Number of Muslims in the U.S. (in millions)

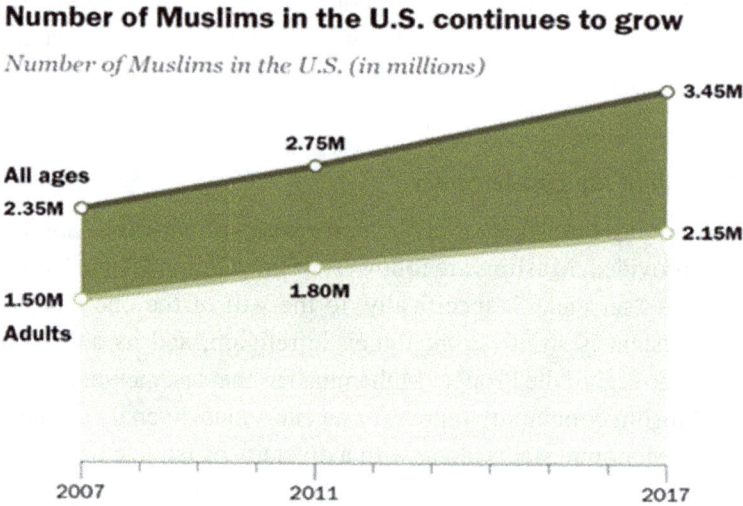

Figure 3: Number of Muslims in the U.S. continues to grow
Source: Per Research Center: 2018

Both PEW and the U.S. Census estimate that their numbers will double by 2050 because of immigration and the high fertility rate among Muslims. In addition, the U.S. Census suggests the U.S. Muslim population will grow faster than the Hindu and Jewish populations in the coming decades, which will make them the second largest religious group in the U.S. by mid-21st century. About two-thirds of the Muslims in the U.S. today (64.5%) are first-generation immigrants (foreign-born), while slightly more than a third (35.5%) were born in the U.S. By 2050, however, more than four-in-ten of the Muslims in the U.S. (46.9%) are expected to be native-born. The top countries of origin for Muslim immigrants to the U.S. in 2010 were Pakistan and Bangladesh. They are expected to remain the top countries of origin for Muslim immigrants to the U.S. in 2050.

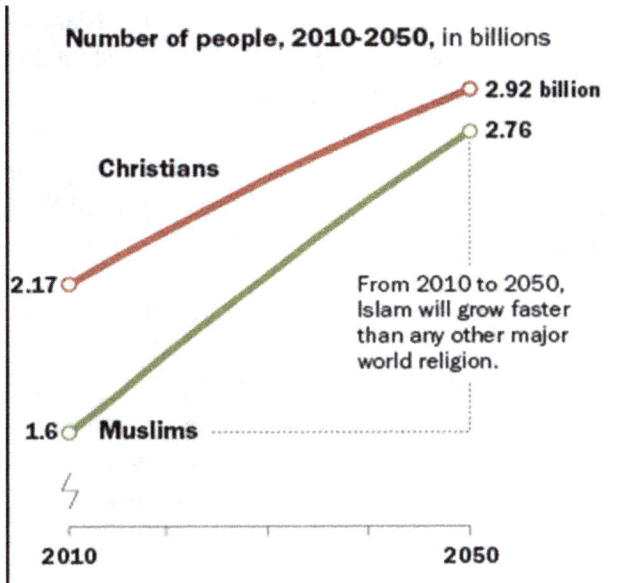

Number of people, 2010-2050, in billions

Christians

2.92 billion

2.76

2.17

From 2010 to 2050,
Islam will grow faster
than any other major
world religion.

1.6 Muslims

2010   2050

Figure 4: Number of people, 2010-2050
Source: The Future of World Religions: Population Growth, Projections 2010-2050

American Muslims come from various backgrounds and are one of the most racially diverse religious groups in the United States. According to the study conducted by the Institute for Social Policy (ISPU, 2017), American Muslims are the only faith community surveyed with no majority race, with 25% identifying as black, 24% as white, 18% as Asian, 18% as Arab, 7% as mixed race, and 5% as Hispanic.

The Muslim population of the United States include Pakistanis, Indians, Bangladeshis, Turks, Palestinians, Syrians, Kurds, Moroccans, Iranians, Iraqis, Bosnians, Kosovo Albanians, Somalis and Afghans, as well as Americans converts – many of them women who have married Muslim men. Estimates of the African-American Muslim population have ranged from about one-fifth to one-third of the total for all Muslim Americans. However, Pakistan is the country where most U.S. Muslims immigrants were born. It is also noteworthy to mention that the experiences of Muslim immigrants and African-American Muslims in the United States are unique in the sense that while they share a common identity as Muslims, their racial, cultural, and historical contexts differ widely. These racial and ethnic differences reflect a host of factors, including the immigrant composition and higher socio-economic status of the South Asian and Arab populations and the long-standing racialized and marginalized position of African

Americans. Indeed, many African Americans converted to Islam seeking a form of religious inclusion they felt lacking in the largely white Judeo-Christian traditions. Most African-American Muslims adhere to mainstream Islamic norms and values, similar to South Asian and Arab Muslim populations. They should not be confused with the Nation of Islam, a group that became popular during the civil rights era by providing a cultural identity that separated black Americans from mainstream Christianity.

Muslim immigrants naturally cluster where others from their homelands already live. Many have settled in metropolitan cities within the states of California, New York, Illinois, New Jersey, Indiana, Michigan, Virginia, Texas, Ohio, and Maryland. There are also established communities near state universities, which often have sizable numbers of foreign-born Muslim students and faculty (PEW, 2014). The overall number of mosques in the United States was 100 in the 1970, but immigration of million of Muslims since then led to hundreds more being built. According to USA Today, the construction of mosques in the United States rose to 2,106 in 2011, and the building boom continues to grow since then (USA Today, 2012). According to Kaleem, by 2016 there were 2600 mosques built in the United States, mostly located in the big states like New York, New Jersey, Florida, California and Texas. The largest mosque, the Islamic Center of America, is located in Dearborn, Michigan **(figure 5 below)**. Many Muslim groups do not have permanent spaces, so only those with a physical building or permanent room that they control were counted. Mosques also had to hold services on Fridays, the main Islamic congregational prayer day, to be counted. While many mosques have historically have been established by South Asian immigrants, newer immigrant groups such as Somalis, Iraqis, West Africans and Bosnians have began to establish their own mosques since 2000 (Kaleem, 2012). According to the Pew Research Center, the number of mosques in the United States rose to 2796 in 2020 (Pew Research Center, 2021). This number reflects the increasing Muslim population in the country as a consequence of recent Muslim migration to the United States. Although the Muslim population has grown in recent years, it still remains a tiny fraction of the American population.

Figure 5: *Islamic Center of America: Dearborn, Michigan*
Source: *islamicsports.blogspot.com*

Socioeconomic status of Muslims

The percentage of U.S. Muslims in individual income and education brackets tracks closely to that of the rest of the U.S. population. According to the PEW survey (2014), Muslim Americans generally mirror the U.S. public in education and income levels, with immigrant Muslims slightly more affluent and better educated than native-born Americans. Twenty-four percent of all Muslims and 29 percent of Muslims have college degrees, compared to 25 percent for the U.S. general population. Forty-one percent of all Muslim Americans and 45 percent of immigrant Muslims report annual household income levels of $50,000 or higher. This compares to the national average of 44 percent. Immigrant Muslims are well represented among higher-income earners, with 19 percent claiming annual household incomes of $100,000 or higher, compared to 16 percent for the Muslim population and 17 percent for the U.S. average (PEW, 2014). This is likely due to the strong concentration of Muslims in professional, managerial, and technical fields, especially in information technology, education, medicine, law, the corporate world, and institutions of higher education. PEW survey show that unlike the low-skilled labor immigration that Western Europe attracted following

World War II, Muslim immigration to the United States during that time was in pursuit of college and advanced degrees that makes their socioeconomic status compatible with the mainstream America. However, some Muslims do live in poverty and have poor English language skills and few resources to improve their situations. The Pew Research Center whose data are widely cited, maintains that immigration and natural population growth gave impetus to the increase, along with the growing financial resources of American Muslims.

Another report published in the September 2021 issue of *the Economist* focuses on Muslims achievements in the United States. This report shows the past 20 years have mostly been golden for American Muslims and Muslims prominence in American life has increased exponentially. Muslims are one of America's most educated groups. More than 15% of doctors in Michigan are Muslims though less than 3% of the state's population is, and more and more artists, journalists and politicians are catching up. The report continues that Muslims like Aziz Ansari, Hasan Minhaj, Ayad Akhtar, and Mahershala are among a generation of award winning actors, writers, and comedians that has emerged in recent years. In politics women like Rashida Tlaib and Ilhan Omar-the first Muslim women in Congress, they are elected onto school boards and into local government (Economist, 2021). As recently as January 20, 2022, President Joe Biden announced the nomination of Nusrat Jahan Choudhury to the federal judiciary Wednesday, who would become the first Muslim American woman to serve as a federal judge. She is also the first Muslim American woman to be nominated to the federal judiciary. Choudhury is currently the legal director at the Illinois division of the American Civil Liberties Union and previously served as the deputy director of the national ACLU Racial Justice Program. She is a graduate of Yale Law School, Columbia University and Princeton University. In addition to a growing occupational and professional diversity among Muslim immigrants in the United States, there is also an increasing number of Muslims engaged in ethnic businesses, running grocery stores, restaurants, discos, and conducting overseas trade in garments and other items. Immigrant-owned businesses began to flourish with the flow of immigration. New positions in these growing small businesses were often filled from the pool of relatives and other family members. Through such economic activities, the family provides not only employment opportunities for new immigrants but also social and economic support in times of need that reflects hard work and motivation to success. The number of Muslim Pakistani American millionaires was reported to be in the thousands. Shahid Khan a Muslim born Pakistani American multi billionaire businessmen owner of the Jacksonville Jaguars of the National Football League

(NFL) making him the first and only ethnic minority member to own one, he also owns English Premier League team Fulham F.C., and automobile parts manufacturer Flex-N-Gate in Urbana, Illinois. This is an amazing achievement by Muslims that after four centuries Islam came to America, the Muslims are finding their place.

In Muslims milieu people can visit each other whenever they desire. Invitation or appointment is not expected for ordinary visits, but sometimes people will phone in advance to make sure that the person is at home. Dishes of various kinds of meats are prepared for the guests. Family rooms are the central place for such occasions. After having exchanged some conversation, women may move to a separate room. However, if visitors are well acquainted with the family then everyone may sit together. They exchange information on different issues. Movies or television shows from home countries are often watched together. Persons from the second and third generation especially like to watch American movies and listen to Western music. Weekend films provided an opportunity to meet and spend time with friends and acquaintances. At these gatherings, people would chat about their work, housing conditions and personal matters. Afterwards, a group of friends might arrange for a collective dinner at someone's home.

Religious status of Muslims

An early survey of Muslim Americans demographic portrait done by the Pew Research Center in 2011 reveals that many Muslim Americans are relatively religious, pray regularly and attend religious services as often as they can, and that Islam plays a very vital role in their lifestyle. The participation of Muslim men in most religious activities is much higher than Muslim women. This is because attendance at weekly religious service (e.g., prayers on Fridays) is mandatory for men but optional for women (Pew Research Center, 2011). Islam sees women as a mother, wife, caregiver, and supporter. Although equality is stressed in the Quran there is a significant gap between men and women's status in many Muslim societies. This gap impairs a woman's economic growth and development, and inequalities in social, religious, and cultural environment.

About the concept of gender equality, the Quran indicates that both men and women are equal. The Quran states:

"Surely, men who submit themselves to God and women who submit themselves to Him, and believing men and believing women, and

obedient men and obedient women and truthful men and truthful women, and men steadfast in their faith and steadfast women, and men who are humble and women who are humble, and men who give alms and women who give alms, and men who fast and women who fast, and men who guard their chastity and women who guard their chastity, and men who remember Allah much and women who remember Him—Allah has prepared for all of them forgiveness and a great reward (Holy Quran, 33:36)".

Here, the Quran is well-defined in stating that men and women are both categorically and clearly equal in their status in front of God, and in expectation of the reward that they are to receive from Him. Had Islam considered men and women unequal, such a verse would not have existed.

Unfortunately, this notion of equality is not reflected in several modern and conservative societies, where Muslim culture is historically male dominated. In many societies gender relations rest on two important cultural perceptions: that man is a dominating figure and is expected to be the guardian of his family, whereas women are responsible for maintaining the family honor and the household with caring and nurturing liabilities. Social and cultural expectations limits women's mobility, places restrictions on their behavior and activities, and permits them only inadequate contact with the outdoor activities. In some Muslim countries such as, Saudi Arabia, Iran, and Afghanistan, women are legally restricted from practicing certain rights. In the United States, gender roles are different. Muslim women have higher educational standards and are working full/part time. They are willing to engage socially and politically in the communities and social services. They have grown into the workforce and out of the role of a stay-at-home mother and housekeeper.

According to Pew Research Center (2017), many Muslims women express their concern about the treatment of U. S. Muslims by some American institutions. A majority of Muslim women say that media coverage of Muslims is unfair and bias. For example, when media portray them as submissive and controlled or unequal and have restricted rights is just a misconception and is not true at all. Muslim women also express more apprehension about anti-Muslim discrimination. Eight-in-ten Muslim women say there are a lot of incidents of discrimination against Muslims. These incidents include having been treated with suspicion, called offensive names, singled out by airport security or other law enforcement, or physically threatened or attacked.

Muslims living in the United States are middle class and mainstream, largely assimilated, happy with their lives and moderate with respect to religion and religious activities. One common trait characterizing Muslim identity is the Five Pillars of Islam mentioned above, which are the framework of the Muslim life. They are the testimony of faith, prayer, giving *zakat* (support to the needy), fasting during the month of Ramadan, and the pilgrimage to Makkah once in a lifetime for those who are able and can afford it. The five pillars are also considered the important acts of worship that develop the Muslim character and strengthen Islam. These acts of worship are performed in the house of worship, which is called a mosque. In inculcating these Islamic beliefs mosques are the center for all Islamic activities. When Muslims from around the world migrated to the United States they adopted a modernist-cum-conservative life style. In order to remain good Muslims and fit into society, they transplant their traditional customs into the American life style. However, doing so is sometimes problematic since the United States' Christian majority dominates the social and political environment. Moreover, Muslim religious routines require facilities that create an inconvenience within non-Muslim surroundings. In their home countries, a close network of mosques provides the location for various forms of Islamic activity, and such religious structures constitute the most obvious reminder of the presence of Islam. In the American context, Muslims were thus eager to build a unifying mosque as a symbol of their community identity. Because religion encompasses strong cultural values, mosque-building activities are quite intensive in these communities. Thus, these mosques are not only places of prayer alone, but also an arena for maintenance of values, norms, and traditions.

The mosques in the United States have a patriarchal structure. Muslim men hold the key leadership positions, namely that of Imam (priest). Among many Muslims there were a growing concern in the community for providing Quranic learning to their children. The mosques also fulfilled ceremonial requirements, and bridge the community together on religious occasions like *Eid* celebrations, prayers and other activities connected with the requirements of religion. Eid is an Islamic name meaning 'Festival' or 'Celebration', and is celebrated throughout the world by all Muslims. It is equivalent to Christians celebrating Christmas. During the whole month of Ramadan, the mosques are very much the center of attention. Imams are invited from other Muslim countries to come celebrate in the United States. The night of power (*Lailatul-qadr in Arabic*) on the 27th of *Ramadan,* the month of fasting *is* especially important since it is thought that the Quran was revealed on that day. The mosques, thus, become the arbiters of tradition in a non-Islamic society in which various social and cultural activities bind them together.

There are two types of *Eids: Eid-ul-fitr* and *Eid-ul Zaha*. Eid-ul-fitr follows Ramadan. Most Muslims go to the mosques for prayer during these holidays. Special food is prepared on this day and everyone wears a traditional garb or hijab. Eid-ul-Azha follows for two and a half months after the Eid-ul-fitr. This day is also celebrated in almost the same way as the first *Eid*. Both Eid's is such a celebration that it brings families and friends closer and people make stronger ties with each other. Everyone invites one another to their homes for foods and exchange gifts and then they go to someone else's house to do the same. Mosques are not only a place of prayer but also a place for seeking Islamic knowledge for Muslims. The mosques along with other cultural and religious centers have become the focus of practicing faith for Muslims, establishing a link with their cultural and religious roots. These institutions are not only a place of religious activities, but are also – and more importantly – an arena for maintenance of norms and values for Muslims. Various social and cultural activities that bind the Muslims are played out in this context. To quote Thomas Jefferson, one of the founders of the nation – that economic and religious liberty and political equality should not be exclusively Christian, but should include every religion practiced in the United States (Spellberg, 2013). This quotation echo strongly not only for religious and economic freedom, but also for what we call an American dream that is the ideal that every American should have an equal opportunity to achieve success and prosperity through hard work, determination, and initiative.

Conclusion

The U.S. Census does not collect information about religions, but estimates on the number of Muslims in the United States range from fewer than two million people to as many as five to seven million. At the highest estimates, the percentage of Muslims in the United States would represent about 2 percent of the total U.S. population as per U.S. Census (2016). A Pew survey from January 2018 shows the figure closer to 3.45 million, including children in 2017, making up roughly 1.1% of the total U.S. population (PEW, 2018). The current population of Muslims is expected to grow rapidly by 2050 because of immigration and higher than average birth rates.

On average, Muslim Americans share similar socioeconomic characteristics with the general U.S. population. They tend to be highly educated, politically conscious and fluent in English. However, some Muslims, and many though not all, African American converted to Islam feel marginalized in socioeconomic domain. Muslims living in the United States are mostly middle class and moderately religious. There is no monolithic Islam that all Muslims adhere to. Religion Islam is diverse Just as Christianity has many different denominations and sects, so does Islam. Muslims are about as religious as are any other Americans. Their frequency of prayer and mosques attendance is moderate to very regular. Just like Christianity and Judaism, Muslims celebrate their religious and cultural festivals that unite and bind them together.

CHAPTER 4

THE NATURE OF ANTI-MUSLIM PREJUDICE: FEAR OR ALARM

Stereotyping Sharia Laws

The most prevalent Islamic prejudice is the development of negative stereotypes in the context of "Sharia Laws", "Jihad", or "Holy War" against the west." This stereotype usually represents violence as an indivisible part of being Islam, as well as presenting religion as justification for violent actions. An example of this kind of stereotype is seen in recent political discourse. President Donald Trump in his election campaign called the religion of Islam as a threat to American values and suggested a ban on Muslims from several countries entry to the United States (Wall Street Journal, 2015). This narrative has been splashed across the front pages of local and national American newspapers throughout the president's election campaign in 2016.

This reflex also resurfaced following the ISIS-inspired attacks in Europe recently. According to the Center for American-Islamic Relations (CAIR), the horrific mass murder in Paris, Belgium and England—perpetrated by people claiming affiliation with the militant group ISIS—has sparked a widespread backlash against Muslims in the U.S., even though virtually every major Islamic group in the country condemned the attacks (CAIR, 2015). Another contributing factor to this marked rise in Islamophobic hostility is the mass media playing on public fears and spreading misinformation about the federal government's ability to screen Syrian refugees from being resettled into the United States. For instance, in 2016, a former GOP presidential candidate named Ben Carson, repeated a discredited conspiracy theory about "jihad," a fantastical plan about a Muslim plot to take over America in the *Mother Jones,* a non-profit news group. When Syrian Muslim refugees became a campaign issue, Carson said, "Bringing in people from the Middle East right now carries extra danger and we cannot put our people at risk because we are trying to be politically correct" (Caldwell, 2016).

It is noteworthy that the desire to be noticed by the media and society, and the ensuing status have been central motive for many of the prejudice attacks on Muslims and other minority groups. In the cases of Donald Trump and Ben Carson, they have indeed become popular among millions of Americans, mainly because of the attention their Islamophobic attack aroused in the media. In many cases, the deliberate objective was to gain such attention, and the people involved who make such radical claims were thrilled when the national newspapers and TV news made stories on them and their disliking of Muslims and Islam.

Dissemination of fear or alarm

The religion of Islam is often unfairly presented as hateful and violent, which leads to a lot of prejudice and hatred towards Muslims in America. Currently, Americans are tending towards less favorable views of Islam which has led to a lot of negativity in American society. While journalists and media in general engage increasingly with their possible contribution to reproducing prejudice, anti-Muslim bigoted images and narratives continue to shape media debates. It should be added that no other faith group is treated with inaccurate and often misleading misrepresentation in the national and social media. Granted, it is understandable that local and national media will highlight the issue of Muslims and Islam in their reporting, given the ISIS terror threat we have seen in recent years. However, there is no reasonable excuse for their deceptions and aggravation in their stories. To address the question whether exposure to media dissemination increases the tendency towards violent behavior? The aforementioned political discourse after 9/11 and later during and after the 2016 presidential elections shows that there is a correlation between exposure to media dissemination and violent behavior, particularly when the issues are related to terrorism and extremism. Many perpetrators of hate violence often act in a political context, with media as a resource to fulfill their objectives. The media often have a direct influence on the actual course of events and their exposure spurs others into action and violence, which we have seen in recent years.

After the 9/11 attacks, many blamed the whole religion of Islam for preaching destruction and violence, without even considering that these hijackers (terrorists) were extreme radicals. In the above-mentioned reference to the Quran, it was explained that the very word Islam is related to a longing for peace and love. A major part of Prophet Muhammad's mission was devoted precisely to bringing an end to the kind of massacre of innocent people, which we witnessed in the 9/11, and subsequent attacks. However, American society does not tend to see this peaceful side of Islam, but rather mostly sees the twisted version of it from Muslim extremists. There are those in American society who see a correlation between terrorism and Islam, yet they fail to understand the idea that there are people who misinterpret scripture and take it to the extreme. Some of these extremists who skew the religion of Islam to tailor their need to kill innocent in order to get their point across are considered fundamentalists who take the idea of conflict to the extreme without even considering a peaceful option such as Islam proclaims.

Finally, it is contradictory that the Quran would call on Muslims to kill or hate all non-Muslims and at the same time preaches for peace and love. The logical conclusion one arrives at when reading the above mentioned versus from Quran is that Islam teaches and encourages Muslims to love all people, including those of different faiths.

Figure 6: Page from Quran
Source: www.pixabay.com

A significant number of Americans of diverse faiths report distrust of and prejudice toward U.S. Muslims, more so than toward any other major faith group studied, (Parillo, 2015). It has become more difficult to be Muslim in the United States in recent years, especially during and after the presidential election in 2016. Islam is often painted as being a religion of hatred and violence in social and political discourse. Several times during and after his presidential campaign Donald Trump said, "I think Islam hates us, and its encourages violence." It is unclear who "us" is since Muslims are Americans as well. He was perhaps reiterating the false notion that Islam teaches Muslims to hate all non-Muslims. The Islamic holy book, Quran provides guidelines and restrictions on the use of violence. The Quran clarifies the relationship between Muslims and non-Muslims as being one that is based on love and compassion. The Quran states, *"Allah does not forbid you to deal justly and kindly with those who fought not against you on account of religion and did not drive you out of your homes. Verily, Allah loves those who deal with equity* (Quran 60: 8)." Furthermore, the Quran highlights the special place of Christians and Jews by constantly referring to them as "people of the book." There are many verses in the Quran that highlight the close relationship between Muslims and non-Muslims. For example, the Quran even prohibits Muslims from insulting the god's or idols that are worshipped by other religions, Although Muslims disagree with non-Muslims who worship any other than God, they are prohibited from insulting or speaking ill of other religious practices. *"And do not insult those whom they call upon besides Allah* (Quran 6:108)." The Quran allows Muslims to eat the food of Jews and Christians and permits interreligious marriage. The Quran states, *"the food of those who have received the Scripture is lawful for you, and your food is lawful for them. And so are the virtuous women of the believers and the virtuous women of those who received the Scripture before you* (Quran 5:5)."

Contrary to the stereotype that Muslims must kill or hate non-Muslims, the Quran notes that Muslims can break bread with people of other faiths. Eating "their" food and non-Muslims eating "your" food implies that there will be a sharing of dinners, occasions, and invitations to each other. The Quran also permits interracial marriages and states, *and (lawful in marriage are) virtuous women of the believers and the virtuous women of those who received the Scripture (Jews and Christians) before you.* This necessitates a friendly and loving interfaith relationship. The concept of marriages among different faith is more compelling. The Quran notes that Muslims can marry women who are Jewish or Christian. Marriage involves love, not only toward the non-Muslim spouse, but also to her family, parents, and siblings. It is contradictory that the Quran would call on Muslims to kill or hate all non-Muslims and simultaneously allow them to marry and share food with them. The logical conclusion one arrives at when reading these verses is that Islam teaches and encourages Muslims to love all people, including those of different faiths.

Unfortunately, and because lack of understanding of Islam, half of Americans, including a large majority of Republicans, say Islam encourages

48

violence. That is twice the number who held that view in 2002. Online surveys conducted by the Pew Research Center in 2016, 2019, and 2021 reveal that Islam is more likely to encourage violence among believers. Republicans and those who lean toward the Republican Party express most reservations about Muslims (Pew Research Center, 2021). "Though we try to assimilate, these are facts we live with and I feel it is harder to be Muslim in the United States today, my God and my religion forbid the killing of any human being, whoever kills an innocent person it is as if he has killed all of humanity." Sheharyar Ali, a Muslim Deputy Attorney in New York told me, while quoting a verse from Quran. A report published in the *Economist* argues that such behavior occurs not only despite the many Muslim paragons, it is also despite America having witnessed astonishingly little jihadist violence. The report further point out that Islamist attacks are reckoned to have claimed 107 lives since 2001, fewer than white supremacists. And nearly half of those causalities occurred in a mass shooting in a gay club which may not have been motivated by religion (Economist, 2021).

The "us vs. them"

The "us vs. them" ideology neither made our world better nor safer. Turning "us" against "them" has definitely helped extremist groups achieve and maintain power as well as reinforce positions of domination and subordination. According to the FBI's Uniform Crime Reports program, annual hate crimes against Muslims are roughly five times higher than the pre-9/11 rate. This is also reflected in a recent survey done by Pew Research Center that shows many Americans believe that Islam encourages hate and violence among believers (see figure 7 below).

The Council on American Islamic Relations (CIAR) is the nation's largest Muslim civil rights and advocacy organization based in Washington, and it reports that ignorance toward Islam and Muslims is widespread in the United States, which partially explains the increase in anti-Muslim attacks in recent years. Ibrahim Hooper, a spokesman for the CAIR, said that he believed the anti-Muslim rhetoric that came out of the 2016 presidential campaign was to blame, and that he feared there would be more hate crimes in coming years.

Americans who say Islam is more likely to encourage violence among believers

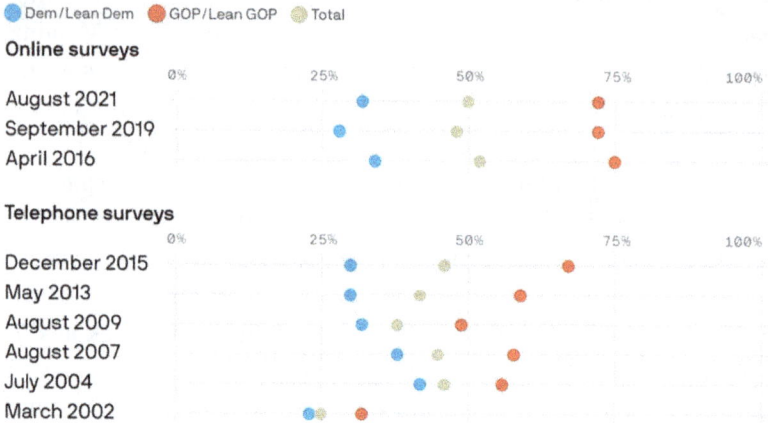

● Dem/Lean Dem   ● GOP/Lean GOP   ● Total

Online surveys

	0%	25%	50%	75%	100%
August 2021		●	●	●	
September 2019		●	●	●	
April 2016		●	●	●	

Telephone surveys

	0%	25%	50%	75%	100%
December 2015		●	●	●	
May 2013		●	●	●	
August 2009		●	●●		
August 2007		●	●	●	
July 2004		●●	●		
March 2002	●●	●			

Figure 7: Americans who say Islam is more likely to encourage violence among believers
Source: Pew Research Center: 2021 Source: Pew Research Center: 2021

"Whenever you have one of the nation's leading public figures in the person of Donald Trump mainstreaming and empowering Islamophobia in the nation, it will be the inevitable result," (CAIR, 2016). Hooper further says that racist, discriminatory activities and Islamophobia are on the rise in the United States, and many hate groups and organizations win sympathy nationwide with "each passing day."

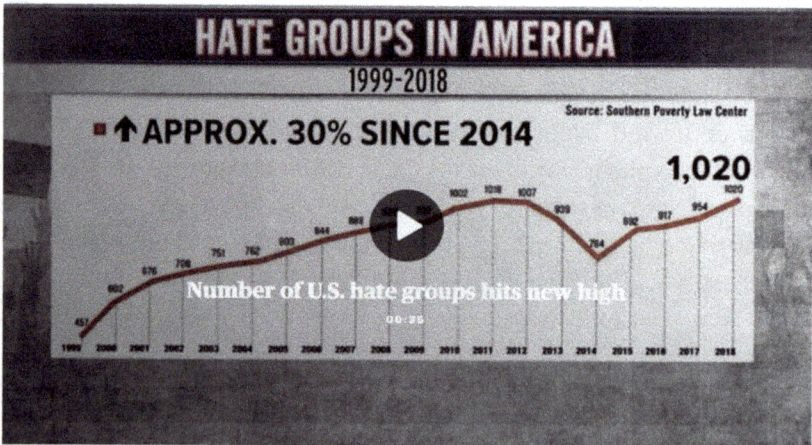

Figure 8: Hate Groups in America
Source: Southern Poverty Law Center

The Southern Poverty Law Center (SPLC) has documented an explosive rise in the number of hate groups since 2000, driven in part by anger by terrorism in the United States and abroad, and demographic projections showing that whites will no longer hold majority status in the country by around 2040. The rise accelerated in 2009, the year President Obama took office, but declined after that, in part because large numbers of extremists were moving to the web and away from on-the-ground activities. In the last few years, in part due to a presidential campaign that flirted heavily with extremist ideas, the hate group count has risen again. In February 2017, the Southern Poverty Law Center (SPLC) released a report highlighting an increase in hate groups across the country, rising from 676 in 2014 to 1020 in 2018 (Mark, 2017) as we have seen in figure above. The Southern Poverty Law Center (SPLC) is a non-profit organization that supports Muslims and racial preferences and defendants' rights, and advocates against what it consider "Islamophobic hate groups". According to SPLC, many violent groups use communicative interaction to promote their extremist ideologies, and to praise those who commit or advocate acts of violence.

The Southern Poverty Law Center has tracked 892 hate groups operating in the United States in 2016, while the most dramatic growth was the near tripling of anti-Muslim hate groups from 5 in 2010 to 34 in 2015, and it has seen a further increase to 101 in 2016 (SPLC, 2016).

Anti-Muslim hate groups and individuals also broadly defame Islam, which they tend to treat as a monolithic and evil religion. These groups generally hold that Islam has no values in common with other cultures, is inferior to the West, and is a violent political ideology rather than a religion. By their rhetoric, they have attempted to establish themselves as the new resistance movement, fighting 'foreign invaders' and present-day political left. For example, people like Robert Spencer, Frank Gaffney, Steven Emerson, and Daniel Pipes speak of 'resistance movement' that will wage a war against the liberal left and its fight against the "Islamization of America." These individuals represent different hate organizations and have been responsible for orchestrating the majority of misinformation about Islam and Muslims in the United States today (C-Span, 2006). Their rhetorical strategies consist of relating themselves to a set of symbols and values which in their original version are held in high esteem by millions of Americans – symbols which represent true nationalism directed against immigrants, particularly Muslims, and with a threat of reprisal against the political left. The language of politics and the media also contributed to this perception. Nayyar Imam, a Muslim community leader in New York told me:

"We witnessed a sharp jump in anti-Muslim incidents nationwide last year, with that spike in Islamophobia continuing through 2016 and accelerating after the November 8 election. Now is the time for those leaders who are concerned about traditional American values of religious inclusion and tolerance to speak out against Islamophobia and anti-Muslim hate crime."

He further said that, "It's deeply worrying to see hate crimes surge in recent years, hate crimes demand priority attention because of their impact on society. They not only hurt victims, but also weaken the bonds of our society." Sheharyar Ali, a Muslim Attorney from New York mentioned above seeks to understand the role of Islam in American constitutional history. He wonders how Islam fits into eighteenth-century American model of religious freedom, when religious suspicion and bigotry was common during the founding of America and thereafter – similar to what is seen today. In her book, *Thomas Jefferson's Quran: Islam and the Founders,* Denise Spellberg argues that politicians like Thomas Jefferson during the founding of the nation believed that American constitution should make room for Islam and the aspect of human rights it represent. Ali argues that contrary to those who defame Islam and Muslims, this enlightened approach of religious liberty might cause these hate groups to rethink what they are saying.

Conclusion

Anti Muslim Racist violence tends to come in patterns of waves or clusters. Such waves of violence have been observed throughout the United States after 9/11 and particularly during Donald Trump's administration. Stereotyping and the negative portrayed of Muslims and the religion Islam is evident in social and political rhetoric.

Spanning across political party lines, the notion of Sharia Laws and the association of "us-versus them" is a concept that perpetuates fear and stereotypes. It is not nuanced, at all. It leads to tragedies like the shooting at Chapel Hill or killing innocent immigrant like Balbir Singh Sodhi discussed below. This also suggests when we perceive that our group is in direct confrontation with another, especially over immigration related issues, we are likely to experience hostility toward members of that group. This perception is reflected in the 2021 Pew Research Center survey that shows many Americans believe that Islam encourages hate and violence among believe.

The concept "us-versus-them" divisions are not only concerned with immigrant status; they often also concern racial categories and ethnic groups such as Arabs and Muslims. As Donald Trump draws a deep line between the white and other minorities, challenging voters in 2020 to declare which side of that line they are on.

The path Trump and his political elite have chosen appears to be one of emphasizing differences and excluding certain groups in the mainstream America. Thus, following this path of creating and emphasizing divisions may be a dangerous way of trying to make America great again.

Islamophobic hate crimes poses a great risk to the democratic foundations of the United States, as well as the coexistence of various cultures, which make America great. Both the political discourse and the civil society should acknowledge the seriousness of this issue and develop concrete strategies to counter Islamophobia. From the outset, there is a need for more face-to-face contact, interaction, and dialogue between Muslims and the host society so as to remove prejudice, alienation, and marginalization. Allport (1954) points out that social cohesion and integration encourage greater social interaction between different communities, which subsequently leads to strong social bonds and more favorable attitudes towards each other. As the founding fathers said:

> *"When we violate one group's freedom, everyone's liberty is at stake. And any attack upon the rights of Christians, Jews, and Muslim citizens should be recognized for what it remains: an assault upon the universal ideal of civil rights promised all believers at the country's founding" (Spellberg, 2013).*

This approach can be tackled successfully if it is supported by national and bipartisan policies that penetrate into societal perception, public discourse, and the sociopolitical landscape. America needs more courageous politicians who do not only speak out against Islamophobia, but also challenge the politics of right-wing populist ideology. Media personnel such as journalists and editors should also challenge Islamophobia reporting in their news media and give space to more balanced views. Generally, the issue of religious knowledge is a huge problem that does not only concern media and politicians, but also the law enforcement agencies and civil society. We see that people simply lack basic knowledge on Muslims and Islam.

The following section is a summary of recent hate attacks against Muslins, based on available statistics and other data on violent acts and perpetrators. Although data are scant, the aim is to establish the extent of the problem, provide a broad overview of trends and patterns of violence.

CHAPTER 5

ISLAMOPHOBIC INCIDENTS AND DEVELOPMENTS IN THE UNITED STATES

Balbir Singh Sodhi; The first victim after 9/11

One of the very first hate crimes followed the September 11th attack, was on September 15th 2001. The victim was Balbir Singh Sodhi, a Sikh American gas storeowner. Balbir was a self-made individual who immigrated to the United States in 1989 and after working hard, made something out of himself and became a business owner. He was shot five times by Frank Roque who mistook him for an Arab Muslim because of the clothes he wore, his turban, and his beard.

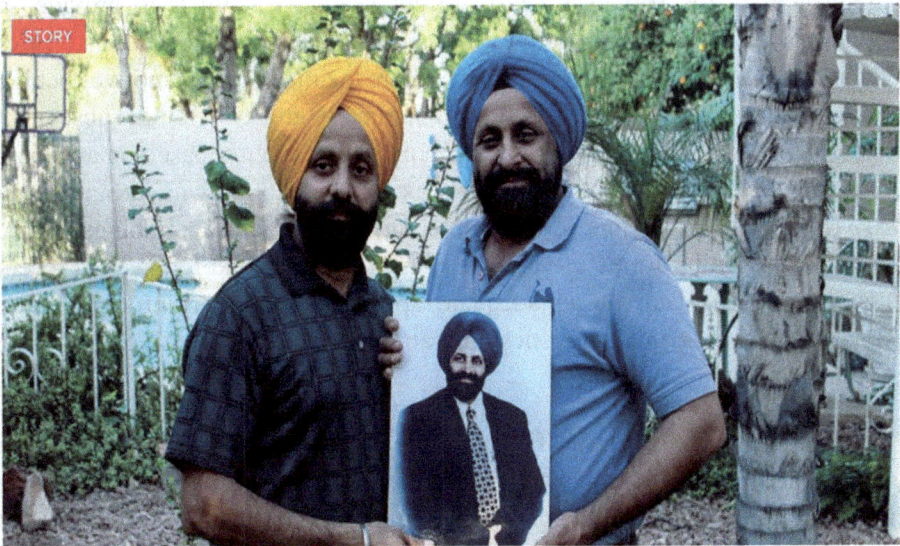

Figure 9: Rana Sodhi (L) and Harjit Sodhi holding a photograph of their late brother, Balbir Singh Sodhi, in Mesa, Arizona
***Source:** Mia Warren for StoryCorps*

Balbir, remembered by many as "Balbir Uncle," grew up in Punjab, in northern India and was a member of the Sikh religion. He left India for the United States after the 1984 anti-Sikh bloodshed. Before opening his gas station, he earned money, much of which he sent home to India, by driving cabs and working the register at a convenience store. Balbir was known to give away candy to the children of customers, who called him "Mr. Bill." He would allow youth to ride their skateboards outside his store, and he'd let people down on their luck fill up for free. Balbir's death marked the first deadly post-9/11 hate crime and kicked off what would become a rising stream of hate incidents against Muslims, Arabs and South Asians.

The story of Texas youth Ahmed Mohamed has become a commonplace exemplification of the deep-rooted realities of Islamophobia in the United States. The 14-year-old Muslim teenager who built a digital clock made out of a pencil case showed it to his schoolteacher. Thinking it was a fake bomb, his teacher informed the police who promptly arrested the youth. This incident happened on June 27, 2016, and has become an ever-present symbol of the bigotry and suspicion that pervades American society regarding its Muslim population.

This section highlights important Islamophobic events, their triggers and consequences in the United States in recent years. The aim is to provide an overview of the main patterns of these Islamophobic acts, and the characteristics of the perpetrators. The section will also explore the rather mixed motives behind their actions, an endeavor which will be continued in greater detail in subsequent sections. The discussion of patterns and perpetrators is partly based on available statistics and chronologies on hate crimes or violence in the United States, and partly from my own attempt to compile comparative data on bombings, arson, shootings and similar forms of violence against Muslims and refugees in recent years. Due to the lack of an adequate apparatus to gather information on Islamophobic events, these statistics only attempt to cover a specific part of the tip of the iceberg.

Since 9/11, the American Federal Bureau of Investigation (FBI) and the Justice Department, have compiled and published, statistics on Islamophobic hate crimes, which are based entirely on voluntary reports by the local law enforcement agencies. As a result of systematic underreporting, there remains enormous gap between FBI hate crime data and the reality of the problem for Muslim Americans and other impacted communities. Therefore, it needs to be done more to collect a reasonable comprehensive and reliable data on Islamophobic acts. The then-FBI director, James B. Comey, acknowledged in a speech to the Anti-Defamation League on May 2017 that the bureau needs "to do a better job of tracking and reporting hate crime, to fully understand what is happening in our communities, and how to stop it" (C-SPAN, 2017).

Recent surge in Islamophobic incidents

The United States has seen a spike in Islamophobic incidents in recent years, with Muslims all over the country falling victim to shootings, personal assaults, harassment, discrimination, and attacks on their houses of worship. In recent years many Muslims have been the victims of a hate crime even with physical altercations in some unfortunate circumstances. This happened to Medinah Academy of Madison's Principal, Umar Warsi on September 21, 2021. Warsi said the following in an interview with NBC News, " we feel like we've had to answer the crimes of other people. I myself have been discriminated against been a victim to hate crime with physical assault, just because I'm Muslim" (Lisignoli, 2021). Warsi's story speaks for the many Muslims that have been a target of a hate group. The motivation of these hate groups is that all Muslims must pay for the crimes of other Muslims that they were never involved with. The murder of two kind Samaritans for aiding two young women who were facing a barrage of anti-Muslim slurs on a train in Portland, Oregon, is among the latest examples of brazen acts of anti-Islamic hatred. Since the beginning of 2017, five different mosques in Texas, Washington, Florida, and Michigan have all caught aflame, and many of the alleged perpetrators have been charged with arson and hate crimes (Yahoo News, 2017). Additionally, in 2016, members of a small extremist group called The Crusaders plotted a bombing "bloodbath" at a residential housing complex for Somali-Muslim immigrants in Garden City, Kansas. Muslim Advocates believe that heated political rhetoric and anti-Muslim policies have emboldened potential vandals. According to Corey Saylor, the director of the Department to Monitor and Combat Islamophobia at the Council of American-Islamic Relations (CAIR), 2016 has been an especially traumatic year for Muslims in America. He said that people who attack American Muslims and their places of worships feel increasingly justified by things such as Donald Trump's proposal to ban all Muslims from entering the United States or his assertion that all of Islam "hates" America (ThinkProgress, 2017).

There are also specific examples of Muslims perceiving negativity against them after 9/11. For example, people who were once kind abruptly no longer talked to or acknowledging the existence of their old Muslim friends. For instances, Samia Omar, Harvard's first Muslim woman chaplain, discussed how her neighbors stopped speaking to her immediately after the attack on the Twin Towers and was even verbally attacked for wearing her hijab. Omar said, "After Sept. 11, everything around you made you feel that you didn't belong here." This demonstrates how the worst prejudice against Muslims came after 9/11 and how prevalent it was. Even though there were particular occasions where a hate crime transpired, Omar stated that everything made her feel as if she didn't belong in America.

Different sources – parallel content

Muslim Americans are grappling with a surge of anti-Islam incidents in recent years across the country, with many hate groups targeting mosques. Most of the incidents are still under investigation, and many constitute hate crimes. Preliminary data from CAIR indicate that 2016 is on track to be the second-worst year on record regarding mosque attacks, and the year 2017 is trailing nearly to the record set by the previous year (CAIR, 2016). The Nation reports that in 2015, 78 mosques were targeted for arson or other forms of vandalism, more than triple the number of mosques targeted in the two years prior (Nation, 2015).

In its annual hates crimes statistics, the Federal Bureau of Investigation (FBI) found that anti-Muslim hate crimes rose by 67%, from 154 incidents in 2014 to 257 in 2015 despite a nationwide drop in hate crimes overall. It was the highest total since 2001, when more than 480 attacks occurred in the aftermath of the September 11 attacks, a staggering 28% increase from the year before. However, the number dropped in the following years, and has never returned to levels reported before the 9/11 attacks. That number was still several times higher than the pre-9/11 levels (figure 10 below). It is also interesting to observe that a spike in such incidents occurs following specific events. For example, in 2015, we found 45 incidents of anti-Muslim crime in the United States in the four weeks following the November 13 Paris terror attack. Just under half of these occurred after December 2, when the San Bernardino terror attack took place. Of those, 15 took place in the five days following December 7, when the then presidential candidate Donald Trump proposed to indefinitely ban all Muslims from entering the United States. In contrast, it is also interesting to note that after an initial sharp spike following the 9/11 attacks, there was a drop in hate crimes after President George W. Bush delivered a speech promoting tolerance, solidarity and mutual contact on September 17, 2001. As you can see from the following figure, right after the speech of the hate crime, incidents dropped sharply from 480 in 2001 to 145 in 2002. This supports what Gordon Allport (1954) concluded in his book, *The Nature of Prejudice*, that meaningful mutual contact with those who are different is crucial for reducing hatred.

Some hate crime statistics

Law enforcement officials acknowledge that the statistics give an incomplete picture, because many local agencies still have a spotty record in reporting hate crimes. Therefore, the data must be interpreted with caution, since unknown number of events may have been missed or gone unreported.

Hate Crime Incidents after 9/11

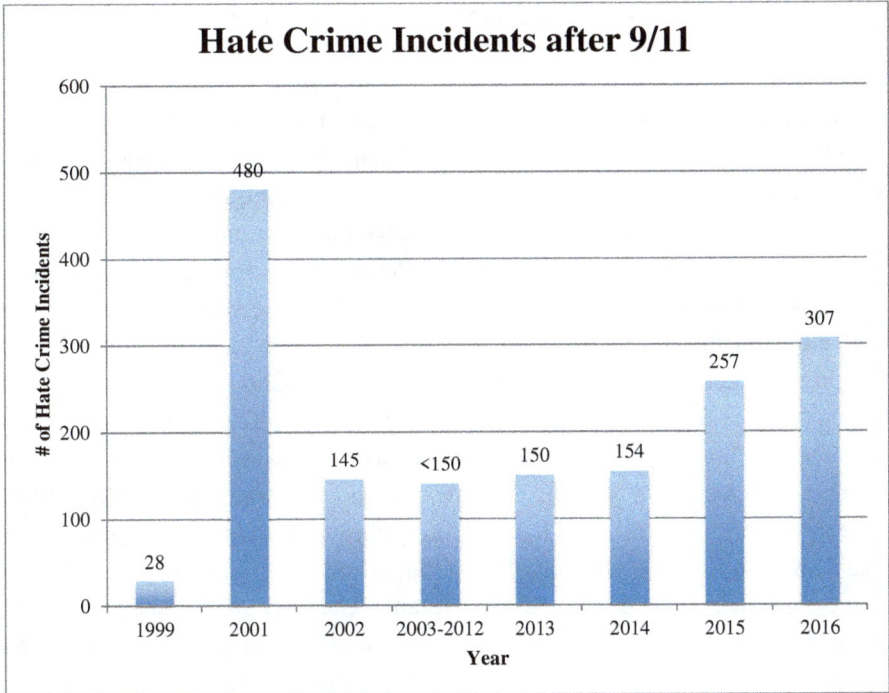

Figure 10: *Hate Crime Incidents after 9/11*
Source: *FBI: The Latest data is for 2016*

The FBI defines a hate crime as a "criminal offense against a person or property motivated in whole or in part by an offender's bias against a race, religion, ethnicity, gender and sexual orientation" (FBI, 2016), whereas the Department of Justice's Bureau of Justice Statistics (BJS) states that an "ordinary crime becomes a hate crime when perpetrators choose a victim because of some characteristics, for example, race, ethnicity, or religion (BJS, 2014). Synthesizing the work of McDevitt et al. (2002) and Perry (2001) discussed earlier, hate crimes typically consist of different factors, such as social, psychological, and contextual, that contribute to hate crime. McDevitt and Bennet (2002) identify that perpetrators are motivated by the "thrill" of their act and the need to enhance their own feelings of power and importance. According to Perry (2001), hate crime is designed to send a message to the victimized community that they are somehow "different" and don't belong" to the wider society". As such, it is a mechanism of power and oppression, intended to reaffirm the role of power dynamic that characterizes a given social order. From this perspective, hate crimes can be seen as verbal abuse through criminal damage, threats, vandalism and act of violence against Muslims and their places of worships. According to the Bureau of Justice Statistics, race is the most common motivation in hate crime, followed by religion and ethnicity (BJS, 2014).

According to Bureau of Justice Statistics, most of the perpetrators are typically men in their late teens and early to mid-twenties who tended to have a low to medium level of education and are predominantly working-class. Most associated with the 2016 presidential elections and look onto Donald Trump as their ideological leader. Trump had heavily focused on minorities, immigrants and Muslims – routinely painting these groups as a threat to economy and national security. Jeb Bush and Ted Cruz, other presidential candidates, had also called for accepting refugees from Syria provided they were Christian, thus effectively banning Muslim Syrian refugees. Yet the fact that only Trump drew widespread outrage shows how accustomed we have become to out-in-the-open anti-Muslim prejudice in this country, and the extremes that now tolerate. "In 20 years, I have not heard such intolerance and hatred from political leaders in this society," told Nihad Awad, executive director of the Council on American-Islamic Relations, to the Guardian in November 2015 (Guardian, December 2015). According to the Southern Poverty Law Center (SPLC), many violent groups use the Internet to promote their extremist ideologies, and to commend those who commit or advocate acts of violence. The Republicans discourse is adding fire to the xenophobia expressed by far-right groups. This is a serious problem that fuels bigotry and hatred (SPLC, 2016).

Perpetrators: Who are they?

The main focus of this study is prevailing anti-Islamic stereotypies by individuals and groups with extreme ideologies and their reasons and rationalization for acting violently against minorities and immigrants. However, there was no firm evidence that these perpetrators were associated with neo-Nazi or racist groups, despite holding apparent racist or Islamophobic views. Although some clusters of violence have been carried out by a single perpetrator or a group of perpetrators as a part of a hate crime, most of these waves do not seem to be coordinated or organized. There is no evidence thus far that large mobs have attacked Muslims and their places of worships. One of the features distinguishing Islamophobic violence from ordinary criminal violence is that perpetrators of such violent acts against Muslims may often find support from other likeminded Americans who are sympathetic to their actions. These actions against Muslims have frequently been preceded by heated debates in the media about terrorism and radical Islam, or issues like Muslim refugees who wished to settle in the United States. Thus, because of the intensive media coverage, perpetrators therefore feel they had a lot of support behind them. In that sense, hate crime may be regarded as an extreme form of an already existing public opinion against Muslims and their religion. The perpetrators could, however, interpret this public opinion as a sign of support that Americans are behind them, unless significant parts of the American population told them otherwise. Interestingly, this has already happened in the form of successful anti-Islamophobic protests and demonstrations, such as "Stop to Islamophobia" and "Defend the Muslim Community" in 2016, and rallies like "I am Muslim Too" in 2017, which gradually spread in the entire country as mentioned and discussed in the previous section.

Conclusion

Islamophobia is not new to the United States. Hate and prejudice against minorities is all too common to the United States since its inception in the early seventeenth century. Many people of different ethnic and racial backgrounds have seen a wave of discriminatory incidents that the Council for American-Islamic Relations (CIAR) called "unprecedented."

Americans need to realize that our nation is becoming multicultural diverse society and that there's no room for stereotyping and prejudice. In some ways, when we hear of a terrorist attack, we automatically think of Islamic people who hold the ideology of seeing America being destroyed. However, American society doesn't realize that these extremists can come from any background or religion. As non-Muslim American citizens approach this serious topic of terrorism, they often find themselves furious in negativity towards Muslims and their religion Islam. Scapegoating Muslims also feeds into the negativity that terrorists groups like ISIS preach, which could ultimately make them stronger if Islamophobia persists. It's up to our nation to create more community alliances with Muslims in the U.S. and abroad so that they can feel less persecuted against. America is the land, which should symbolize safety and security for anyone, no matter what background he or she comes from.

Although the FBI publishes statistics detailing its hate crime investigations, no federal agency tracks reports of hostilities against Muslims. What is more, the FBI's reports only include the most serious incidents, such as homicides and stabbing. The FBI acknowledges that the statistics they provide is an incomplete picture of Islamophobic incidents, since it is very likely that most Islamophobic incidents go unreported. But looking from an objective perspective, the FBI'S statistics does provide a small window into the discrimination that American Muslims face every day.

Finally, individual perpetrators and groups of hate crime may be divided into various distinctive types, which vary in terms of social background, motivation, and behavior, as described by McDevitt and Perry. They identify that perpetrators are motivated by the "thrill" of their act since many of them told the police that they were just looking for some fun. The perpetrators reported further that they left their own neighborhood to search for a victim in a place of worship in another part of town, or a minority neighborhood. The target was chosen because the perpetrator perceived that the victim was in some way significantly different from the perpetrator.

Thus, over the past few years, Islamophobia has increased immensely. With various terrorist attacks occurring over the year, it has left deep concern for the future and how religious hate crime offences are increasing. There are different ways for improving the outcomes of religiously aggravated hate crimes, one being passing a stronger message that every person is equal and that hate crime against any group will not be tolerated and accepted. This could be done through media, public policy, or how the criminal justice system treats people of different religions and how the police stereotype when they perform stop and searches. Another factor to reduce prejudice is through strengthening the ways to fight hate speech in public and social forum, making it clear to people that social media will not be used to incite hate crime.

The following chapter focuses on the role of the mainstream media's coverage of attack on Muslims and their religion, Islam. Does exposure to media violence increase the tendency towards violent behavior? Although I have tried to address the issue briefly, the question is far too general to be answered in this study.

CHAPTER 6

THE ROLE OF THE MEDIA AND ISLAMOPHOBIA

Figure 11: The Universal Role of Media
Source: *American Press Institute*

Defining media

Media is exerting increasing influence on the today's society. Media is a collective term that refers to the main modes of broadcasting and communication used in the present-day. The development of mass media through technology has enabled an easy access for people to the most recent events and news at the click of a button. Media can range from television to news articles to the Internet and social media platforms, such as Twitter, Facebook, LinkedIn, Instagram, and many more. Media coverage tends to focus on the most pressing social issues and events, including Islamophobic hate, which is the topic of this paper. Mass media can be broadly classified into the print media (newspapers and magazines) and the broadcast media (radio and television). Although most Americans used to obtain their news from newspapers and magazines, electronic journalism, particularly TV and online journalism, has become dominant in the last 50 years. Today, technological advances have facilitated rapid access to information via

63

Internet and social network platforms that reach large numbers of people in a very short time.

The media narratives promoting anti-Muslim rhetoric are some of the main causes of Islamophobia amongst the general American public today. The negative portrayal of Muslims and Islam plays a significant role in shaping the misguided beliefs regarding Islam and Muslims in broader civil society. Social media, as well as highly rated TV channels, reproduce such stereotypes by engaging in a debate on cultural explanations for violent attacks on Muslims. For instance, Fox News's Bill O'Reilly stated Islam "a destructive force and that the United States is in a holy war with certain groups of Muslims" (Fisher, 2015). Thus, the impact of media and negative beliefs held by the general population fuel more biased viewpoints towards Muslims that, in turn, incite violent behavior and support perpetrators. Below, some official statistics and underreporting of hate crimes by the media and the victims themselves are discussed

The Islamophobic media: Underreporting

The role of the media in the rise of anti-Muslim rhetoric in the United States is obvious. In the past few years, the American media have subjected groups and individuals to hate crime. According to the Center for American-Islamic Relations (CAIR, 2015), the rise in hate crimes and bias incidents began after Nov. 13, 2015, when gunmen belonging to the Islamic State in Iraq and Syria (ISIS) opened fire in Paris, killing 130 people. The number of reports spiked further after a Muslim couple, who reportedly pledged allegiance to ISIS, killed 14 people a mass shooting in San Bernardino, California, on Dec. 2, the same year. Further attacks in Belgium and the UK perpetrated by people claiming affiliation with the militant group ISIS-sparked a widespread backlash against Muslims in the U.S., even though virtually every major Islamic group in the country condemned these attacks. Figures released by the Federal Bureau of Investigation (FBI, 2017) in November 2017 show that between 2015/16 and 2016/17 the number of hate crimes against Muslims increased to 307, i.e., by more than 100% compared to less than 150 before 2014. This begs the question if media does more harm than good in preventing incidents such as hate crimes. It seems that the media is always portraying these situations in biased ways and takes sides mainly to keep the viewers entertained. It is even more worrying to note that hate crime is underreported in the official figures. This can happen because of race or the fact that people could fear going to the police and be charged or accused wrongfully if they belong to a minority group.

The Department of Justice (DOJ, 2017), a major regular monitor of these trends, anticipated that many incidents of hate crimes were not reported to the police between 2011 and 2015 and that hate crime rates were the highest in urban areas, especially in the west (Yadidi, 2017). The DOJ defined hate crimes as those that manifest evidence of prejudice based on rage, gender or gender identity, religion, disability, sexual orientation or ethnicity. On the contrary, Southern Poverty Law Center (SPLC, 2016) found that many immigrants who were victims of hate crime chose not to report the incident to the police because they were afraid that their claims would not be taken seriously, or could even result in incarceration because they are a minority group.

These trends are truly worrying. As discussed in the section below, Islamophobic hate crimes are presented in the media in a way that can sometimes instigate hate crimes and support perpetrators.

The manifestation of Islamophobia in the media

Media coverage of Islam and Muslims in the Western world has changed dramatically since the beginning of the 21st century. The events of September 11th, 2001, thrust Islam into the global media forefront, due to which not only coverage of Islam drastically increased, but the way in which Islam was framed by the media changed as well. The use of the term "Jihad" and calling terrorists "Jihadists" was promoted by the media. The same bias is present when naming terrorists "Islamist militants" or "Islamist fundamentalists," creating an impression that Islam is a violent religion. Media has drawn attention to the issue, but has often incorrectly portrayed people and events in biased ways.

In 2009, Mehdi Hasan, a British journalist and broadcaster, criticized Western media for over-reporting a few Islamist terrorist incidents but underreporting the much larger number of planned non-Islamist terrorist attacks carried out by white perpetrators (The New Statesman, 2009). According to a study published in *Justice Quarterly* in 2017 by students at Georgia State University, "controlling for target type, fatalities, and being arrested, attacks by Muslim perpetrators received, on average, 357% more coverage than other attacks".

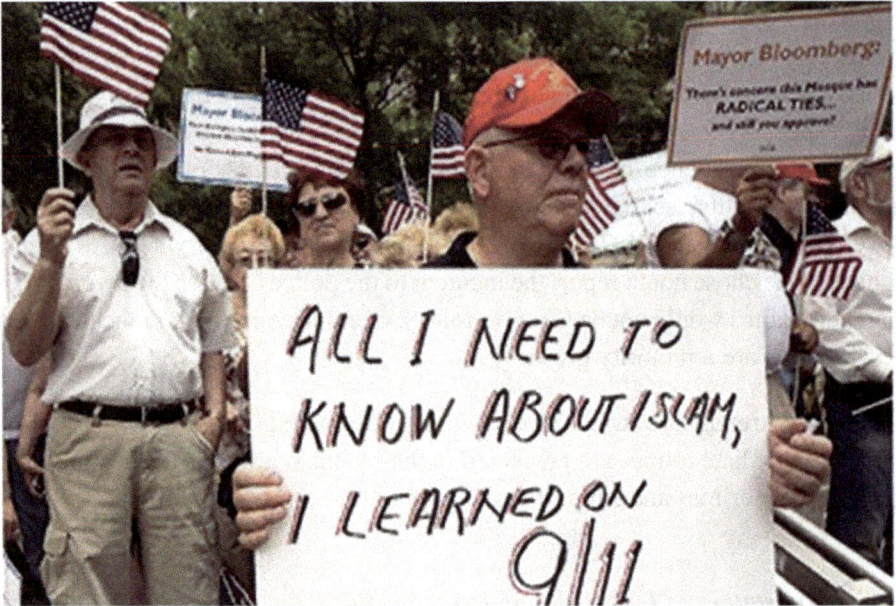

Figure 12: Supporters of the Tea Party movement
Source: www.aattp.org

The study highlights one-sidedness in news coverage, such as the sheer amount of coverage granted to the small number of domestic terrorists who were both Muslims and from outside of the U.S. The authors further noted that, in the United States, members of the public tend to fear "Muslim terrorists" while ignoring other threats (Kearns, Betus, & Lemieux, 2019).

Muslims, as a minority in the United States are often singled out and discriminated against on the basis of their religion and ethnicity. According to Parillo (2015), in 2012, Americans felt least socially associated with and therefore socially distant from Arabs and Muslims. Over the past few years, there has been an increase in hate crimes and prejudice against Muslims in the U.S. owing to the terrorist attacks, the election of President Trump, and the long-existing stereotypical images of Muslims (Edwards & Rushin, 2018). Similarly, in another recent study conducted on representation of Muslims in media from 2000 to 2015, Ahmed and Matthes (2016) found that Muslims are generally negatively framed, whilst Islam is characterized as an intolerant and violent religion. British scholars Egorova and Tudor (2003) cited other European researchers in suggesting that expressions used in the media such as "Islamic terrorism," "Islamic bombs," and "violent Islam," while not using the same terms relating to non-Muslims, have resulted in a negative perception of Islam. There have also been examples in the movie industry in which Muslims were associated with terrorism, such as in the 1998 movie *The Siege* and the 2018 popular TV program *Bodyguard,* which focused on Islamic terrorism. Some critics have stated that the manner in which Islam is portrayed in the entertainment industry only furthers the stereotype that Muslims are correlated with terrorism and savagery.

The American media began adopting the term "Islamophobia" after 9/11 attacks in order to describe the rise in negative feelings towards the Muslim community. Since then, the term "Islamophobia" has been in prevalent usage both in academia and in the public discourse. Islamophobia operates by creating static "Muslim" identity, which is associated with negative terms and generalized for all Muslims. Erik Bleich (2011) described this harmful rhetoric as indirect promotion of harmful actions against Islam and Muslims in Western democracies. The American doctrine on "War on Terrorism" led to an increase in Islamophobia in the United States and across the globe. This was in turn reflected in the way media outlets portrayed and stereotyped Muslims and Islam. This is especially problematic because of the growing influence the media has on the population's perception-forming process. While some media deliberately frame Islamic coverage positively in an attempt to counter Islamophobia, many of the portrayals of Muslims contribute to the formation of harmful Islamophobic stereotypes. Hate crimes are presented in the media in a way that can sometimes incite hate crimes and support perpetrators. This was the case for Antonia Martinez, who called himself Muhammad Hussein, and was allegedly a Muslim man planning to blow up a Baltimore military recruitment center. He pleaded guilty and sentenced to 25 years in federal prison (Bishop, 2012). Extensive articles were written about this case in the national media.

The coverage of his trial spurred further Islamophobia in the United States and seemed to legitimize existing prejudice against Muslims. Because of the widespread reporting on Martinez's case, Many Americans were exposed to message about "terrorist Muslims" and was led to believe that they are threat to the national security. The influence of social media in instigating widespread develops social prejudice against Islam and the Muslims will be discussed next.

Social media and the online factors

Social media plays a significant role in everyday life of majority of people. The online media outlets allow for a new way to reach a large number of users, as well as to target specific individuals. As a result, campaigns of prejudice and harassment now have online as well offline dimensions (Miller, 2015). The fact that one does not even have to know or be in physical proximity to the person to be able to abuse or harass them makes social media so popular among those promoting hate crimes (Goldman, 2018). As online communication has become so ubiquitous, individuals inclined toward racism or homophobia have found niches that can reinforce their views. Social media platforms also offer these perpetrators the opportunity to publicize their acts. According to Laub (2019), strong correlation exists between online hate speech and hate crime incidents caused by social media websites such as Facebook and YouTube. For example, a hate group can specifically target those with similar interest, thus facilitating recruitment. In addition, social media users can access videos and websites that promote their racist ideologies. In that sense, social media supports or catalyzes hate crimes. Individuals that already hold racist or homophobic beliefs find content and other like-minded people that reinforce their views, which can eventually lead them to violence. As a part of this investigation, Laub (2019) conducted a comparative analysis of the relationship between social media and hate crimes in different countries. He found that, in several domestic terrorist attacks, social media played a significant role in bringing the perpetrator closer to realizing his goals. For example, in the United States, white supremacists often circulate in online racist communities. In instances such as the Charleston Church shooting in 2015 and the Pittsburg Synagogue shooting in 2018 in which several innocent people died, the perpetrators had spread their beliefs online and had been led to believe that violence was the ultimate requirement of white supremacy, mostly through viewing online content that reinforced their prior beliefs (Laub, 2019). Social media also acts as a tool of inspiration, as illustrated by the 2019 mosque shooting in Christchurch, New Zealand, which was broadcast live on Facebook, Twitter, and other media outlets. The perpetrators had posted their manifesto online that had reached a global audience. Fortunately, after this incident no more hate crimes of significant nature occurred in New Zealand or the United States.

This analysis highlights the significant role that social media plays in facilitating hate crimes. It provides perpetrators with easy access to like-minded individuals, increasing the pool of people willing to act on their beliefs. As perpetrators can rapidly disseminate their manifestos via online platforms, social media has provided the means to inspire others. For example, Patrick Koegan from Massachusetts threatened to burn down a local mosque on Facebook because he was inspired by other terrorist attacks in the United States in which local mosques were burned down or attacked. In his Facebook post in response to an attack on Islamic Center in Missouri on July 14th, 2013, Keogan posted, "Somewhere out there is an unknown hero. The people's champion, a true God amongst mortal men. May your days be many and trouble be few my good man" (Main, 2018). This Islamophobic rhetoric and praise of a terrorist shows that Keogan felt inspired by the media coverage to copy prior terror attacks against Muslims.

Biased media coverage and social prejudice contribute to the negative portrayal of minorities in the Media outlets promote hate crimes and support perpetrators by creating false perceptions of minorities, making a distinction between the portrayal of victims and the perpetrator, and exaggerating crime rates among minorities Islamophobic comments are promoted by journalists as well as broadcasters, with right-wing extremists invited onto news and programs on a regular basis, often without being challenged about their Islamophobic perception. Sadly, following ratings seems to be more vital than acquiring balance and objective approach.

Figure 13: *Islamophobia in the news outlet*
Source: *Centre for Analysis of the Radical Right*

The way in which the media portrays minorities creates a perception that puts a target on certain groups, ultimately leading to perpetuation of stereotypes. Using the terms "terrorism," "fundamentalists," "terrorists," "extremist," and "backward" in connection to Islam and Muslims incites prejudice against

Muslims and their religious congregation. This is aptly exemplified by the case of Marq Vincent Perez from Texas who burned down the Victoria Islamic Center in 2017, the only mosque in his hometown Victoria. Perez had believed that the members of the mosque were terrorists and were planning a terrorist attack in the near future (Lichtblau, 2017). Of course, Perez had no evidence of the Muslim community planning another attack, but his suspicion turned him into a radical terrorist, which led him to commit act of terrorism against the Muslims in his hometown.

Perez's unfounded hatred of Muslims and Islamophobia was likely instigated by the media that continuously reports on ISIS and Jihadist Muslims, which stereotypes Muslims as dangerous and radical terrorists. This stereotype has incited fear among Americans like Perez whose intense distrust of all followers of Islam prompts them to act out of fear and hatred. Ted Hakey of Meriden from New Hampshire similarly fired gunshots at a local mosque in November of 2015, motivated by learning of the terrorist attack in Paris in which 130 people lost their lives. This demonstrates that the way minorities are portrayed in the media has a strong effect on societal perceptions of those specific groups, which can ultimately lead to an increase in hate crimes.

According to the report published by the All Party Parliamentary Group on Hate Crimes (APPGHC, 2018), negative portrayal of minority groups in the media qualifies as "abuse, and as cause of abuse". In other words, when a specific minority group that is already portrayed negatively in the media, whether through enforcing stereotypes or otherwise, this gives perpetrators an excuse and ultimately a justification to commit a hate crime against said minority.

The news media plays a key role in shaping societal values and has a significant influence on individual attitudes and behaviors. In the United States, Muslims are discussed more negatively than other minority groups across different social spheres. Muslims and Islam are often associated with terrorism and aggression, especially after 9/11 attacks, and this has led to an increase in negative sentiments and the enforcement of stereotypes and discrimination. According to Howard (2019), this incites anti-Muslim sentiments and thus increases hate crimes against this group. In sum, the media plays an important role in promoting prejudice against Muslims by portraying them negatively, as it inspires already prone perpetrators to increase harmful activity, using those negative portrayals as a justification for their actions.

Media coverage of Islamophobic bias: Main trends

Media representation of Islam and Muslims particularly after 9/11 is an engaging and exciting case study. The problem is that media highlights negative news involving Muslims more than positive news. The absence of positive and more representative and balanced stories helps people form stereotypical opinions of Islam. The way in which Islamophobic offenses are reported in the U.S. media is also highly problematic. Instead of focusing on the majority of offenses that occur in the U.S., media tends to report on attacks that seem to be committed by Islamic groups or individuals who affiliate themselves with Islam. Generally, perpetrators perceived as Muslims receive twice the media coverage as their non-Muslim counterparts for being involved in hate crimes or other violent acts, whereas for cases of terrorism they receive seven and a half times as much media coverage (Rao et al., 2018). In his article on Islamophobia in the U.S. media, Oded (2018) highlighted that terrorist attacks committed by Muslims received 105 headlines in national news outlets, compared with merely 15 covering attacks committed by non-Muslims. Similarly, in their more recent study on news coverage on all terrorist attacks committed in the United States between 2011 and 2015, Kearns et al. (2019) found that attacks by Muslim perpetrators received 449% more coverage than attacks carried out by non-Muslims. It is evident that, by giving more publicity to attacks committed by Muslim perpetrators, the media is implying that these incidents are much more common.

The terms used to describe acts of violence of non-Muslim and Muslim perpetrators are also very different. For example, when a Muslim individual has been involved in an act of violence, this is invariably described as a terrorist attack stemming from Islamic ideology, which is then attributed to the entire community. When a non-Muslim is involved, the act is typically blamed on the individual and their state of mind. Similarly, Christian rightwing extremist and other violent acts of racism are excluded from the category of "terrorism." For example, the Oklahoma City bomber Timothy McVeigh was tried for domestic terrorism and sentenced to death but the trial coverage did not focus exclusively on his crime against humanity. Media focused on McVeigh's social life and his supposed loneliness, inability to fit in, and problems with girls in high school, as well as his military career. In short, there was an odd aspect of sympathy for the perpetrator of this immense tragedy. The media portrayed him as a troubled white teen with serious volatile issues that made him upset, which is in stark contrast with Antonio Martinez's (alias Muhammad Hussein) case mentioned earlier who was described as a terrorist and a violent person who wanted to harm Americans.

In his article about the detrimental effects of Fox News racial reporting, journalist Brian Powell stated (2013), that Fox News racial crime coverage is hurting people because they perpetuate harmful racial stereotypes. As pointed out by Powell, Muslims are constantly being portrayed in the news as suspicious or affiliated with terrorism and its sympathizers, the social consciousness shifts to favor the more prevalent negative image of Islam and the Muslims.

Most news coverage of Muslims in American media is negative

In his book, *Islamophobia in the Media since September 11th*, Allen (2010) cited a sample of news that emerged after 9/11, which clearly indicated that Muslim viewpoints were underrepresented and that issues involving Muslims usually depicted them in a negative light. Such portrayals, according to Allen, include the depiction of Islam and Muslims as a threat to Western security and values. As the author noted, "Whilst some media sources and publications have tried to act with responsibility in realizing the implications of such discrimination, certain specific and often predictable sources have been actively incorporating the most explicit expressions of Islamophobia into their coverage deeming their actions irresponsible, prejudicial, insightful and more directly, extremely dangerous" (Allen, 2010).

Bill Maher, a popular media personality and a host of the political satire program "Real Time with Bill Maher" on HBO consistently demonizes and stigmatizes the Muslim community despite his claim to hold progressive and tolerant opinions. He has frequently spoken against Islam and its believers, saying, for example, "Islam is the motherlode of bad ideas, the Quran is a hate-filled holy book and the Islamization of Europe is underway" (Cohen, 2017). CNN has for a long time promoted a kind of "he said, she said" conception of Islam, suggesting that it is valid and worthwhile to debate whether Muslims make for inferior people and societies, thus mainstreaming more overt bigotry. CNN host Chris Cuomo, for example, called Muslims "unusually violent" and "unusually barbaric." The network has run chyrons such as "Is Islam Violent? or peaceful?" When CNN came under fire for asking if Islam promotes violence, several hosts countered that they were just following their journalistic responsibility to "ask the question." In other cases, the media has spread stories based on half-truths and distorted facts, often uncritically accepting or misrepresenting "facts" provided by the law enforcement agencies, politicians, or Islamophobic groups and individuals. Other U.S. TV networks and some of their anchors and presenters have often produced images, which are liable to incite fear and anxiety among many Americans. For example, Mike Huckabee, one of the Fox News Channel hosts, falsely claimed that Muslims believe that "Jesus Christ and all the people who follow him, are a bunch of infidels who should be essentially obliterated." Huckabee also referred to Islam as the "antithesis of the gospel of Christ" (William, 2013). Fox News has taken this media treatment of Islam to the next level by repeatedly telling millions of its viewers that Muslims are a threat that must be feared and dealt with forcefully, even violently. For example, Bill O'Reilly has declared that "Islam is a destructive force", and that the U.S. is in a holy war with certain groups of Muslims (Fisher, 2015).

The myth of "Islamization" on media: Political rhetoric

In the U.S. and other Western countries, Muslims tend to be associated with "Sharia laws," "jihad," or "holy war against the West. Many examples of this kind of rhetoric can be found in recent political discourse. President Donald Trump in his 2016 election campaign called Islam as a threat to American values and suggested surveillance of mosques and ban on entry to the United States for all Muslims. Such anti-Muslim rhetoric works to exacerbate the fears and misconceptions among U.S. citizens, as they are led to believe that all Muslims are a threat to national security.

In 2016, Ben Carson, a former GOP presidential candidate, in an interview given to the nonprofit news organization *Mother Jones*, referred to a discredited conspiracy theory about "jihad"—a fantastical plan about a Muslim plot to take over America. When Syrian Muslim refugees became a campaign issue, Carson said, "Bringing in people from the Middle East right now carries extra danger and we cannot put our people at risk because we are trying to be politically correct" (Caldwell, 2016). While giving an interview on CNN in November of 2015, Ben Carson compared Syrian refugees to rabid dogs stating, "If there's a rabid dog running around in your neighborhood, you're probably not going to assume something good about that dog, you're probably going to put your children out of the way. That doesn't mean that you hate all dogs" (Scott, 2015). "As Carson was in favor of extreme vetting process for Syrian refugees, he added, "We have to have in place screening mechanisms that allow us to determine who the mad dogs are. Quite frankly, who are the people who want to come in and hurt us and destroy us" (CNN, 2015)? Among his many false claims, it is worth noting that Ben Carson argued that, according to the Islamic law, people following other religions must be killed.

John Bolton, senior fellow at American Enterprise Institute, also made a blatantly false and misleading statement regarding refugees, claiming, "It's not merely this wave of hundreds of thousands of refugees into Europe and ultimately into the United States that poses the threat. It's even if they're not radicalized when they leave they can be radicalized at a distance" (Nazarian, 2015). Newt Gingrich, another established politician and the former speaker of the United States House of Representatives, believes that Sharia is the "mortal threat to the survival of freedom in the United States and we should deport any who believe in Sharia law" (CAIR, 2016).

Why do editors and newscasters allow such words to be published or spoken without question? The simplest answer probably is that the stories that play on the public's fears and feed their prejudices are popular. Some politicians exploit the mass media's criteria of 'newsworthy' event. As freelance writer and blogger Woolfe (2018) argued, "the media uses bold and harsh language to promote this kind of fear because bad news sells" The media is often biased and the coverage of anti-Islamic hate crimes is often not highlighted. Muslim viewpoints are underrepresented and issues involving Muslims are usually depicted in a negative light. In his book *Covering Islam: How the media and the experts determine how we see the rest of the world*, Said (1997) commented that, in reality, the biases which inform the media coverage of Muslims and Islam date back to the development of an anti-Islamic orientalist discourse, which constituted the identity of the West and continues to shape its discourse. This discourse is premised on the idea of Western superiority and the inferiority of the "rest" because the West is portrayed as the birthplace of democracy, rationalism, and science. In other words, as West is highly advanced in every respect, the "rest" are dependent on the "West" (Said, 1997).

Evaluation of media coverage of Islamophobia

The term "Islamophobia" gains its significance post September 11, 2001. Shortly commemorate the victims and demonstrate their patriotism. It was a beautiful sunny day when I came home from the school where I was undertaking my Ph.D. studies, where I found my three daughters depressed and emotionally upset because of the attacks on the twin towers one of the most chaotic days in American history. My eldest daughter, Maira said, dad, "We just had an aircraft hit the World Trade Center. I started to console her by saying that just pray to God that American is safe. Then she pointed me to the TV screen in the sitting room. You could see people were jumping from the building and smoke pouring out everywhere. I was lost in my thoughts wondering how could someone hit World Trade Center." It was beyond my imagination. It was quite a bit silence in the room and then suddenly my daughter said, "Dad, we want an American flag." I took them around the city, but did not find any flags in shops – I couldn't buy even one flag for my daughters. All the American flags were sold out that day. This was the situation in New York, my city where I lived for so many years after migrating from Norway. The emotions in the city were high and everything looked lifeless. People were mourning. People attended candlelight vigils and participated in moments of silence.

After 9/11, most Americans thought that Islam was the cause for such horrific crimes, their grief manifested itself as anger and frustration, and they looked for someone to blame for the attacks. As a consequence, hate crimes towards Muslims increased. Anger erupted into attacks on people of Arab and Muslim descent, with nearly several incidents in the first 30 days after the attacks. A man on an anti-Muslim rampage in Arizona fatally shot a gas station owner, Balbir Sigh Sodhi who was an Indian-born Sikh, mentioned earlier in the book. This type of confusion was not uncommon, since many Sikhs wear turbans, have beards and are seen as looking like Muslims.

Muslim women in particular have been targeted because a number wear the hijab, said Samia Omar, Harvard's first Muslim woman chaplain. Omar, who had moved from Egypt to New York City in 2000, remembers how her neighbors stopped talking to her the day after the attacks. "After Sept. 11, everything around you made you feel that you didn't belong here," said Omar, who was verbally attacked for wearing a hijab. "It's been 20 years, since 2001 to 2021, and we still have the same fear and the same concerns," said Omar (The Harvard Gazette, 2021).

The term Islamophobia became prominent on the media after 9/11 attacks. The term continuously being shared on the Internet and via emails and text message, as well as other social media networks. Overall, the media has had a negative portrayal of Islam and Muslims over the past few years and particularly after the elections of 2016 when Donald Trump took office. Such anti-Muslim portrayal and sentiments spread quickly because of misleading and in accurate information about Islam by the media to its audience.

MediaTenor, a research institute that evaluates data for NGOs and governments, analyzed the reporting practices of Fox News, NBC, and CBS in the 2007–2015 period to determine how Islam was represented by these major media outlets. Their findings revealed that over 80% of the media coverage on NBC and CBS was negative, while over 60% of the coverage on Fox was unfavorable, with stories about international terrorism and conflict getting the most airtime (Habib, 2016). In addition, the researchers found that, in most cases, Muslims were not included in the TV programs as featured experts on Islam. This perception towards Islam and Muslims is closely linked to media portrayals of Islam as an irrational, primitive, and violent religion.

Media reports in recent months have indicated a continued flow of attacks, often against victims wearing traditional Muslim garb or seen as Middle Eastern. James Nolan, a former FBI crime analyst who teaches about hate crimes at West Virginia University, stated that the available data seemed to show "a real spike" in hate crimes against American Muslims, caused in part by political and social discourse (New York Times, 2016). Mark Potok, a senior fellow at the Southern Poverty Law Center (SPLC), which monitors hate groups and extremism, went further to assert, "I don't have the slightest doubt that Trump's campaign rhetoric has played a big part" in the rising attacks (SPLC, 2016).

In her article, Vox founder and Journalist Ezra Klein examined how the media portrays president Donald Trump's blatant racist attitudes. Transparency, as Klein (2019) suggests, is extremely valuable, as public needs to be conscious of the political attitudes of those in power. This idea, when examined at its most basic form, shows how important it is to cover news in understanding manner. It is noteworthy to many Americans that Trump is racist and has certain biases against minorities. His policies are a clear reflection of his ideas about other people unlike him. But there is another more sinister consequence of such transparency, as broadcasting Trump's negative views can serve as a constant signal to racists that their views are condoned by the U.S. society at the highest level (Klein, 2019). This is also a fact that there is quite a lot Trump says about different groups in our society that the media, both the mainstream media and social media — overlooks.

When on one occasion Trump was asked about criticisms that his comments were often racist, Trump replied, "It doesn't concern me because many people agree with me." Commenting on his rhetoric, Nayyar Imam, a Muslim-American community leader and a chaplain mentioned elsewhere in the text said, "It was disappointing that such a prominent American figure, especially one running for president at the time, could say such defamatory things about an entire religious group. Trump should read up on the Constitution, and stop this hatred. No matter who it is, Muslims or any other religious community, enough is enough. You are going for a leadership position. Act like a leader and know that America is built on immigration and people with diverse backgrounds."

Conclusion

It is too simplistic to assume that the media incite hate crimes and supports hate groups and perpetrators. The finding in this chapter indicate that media coverage can have effects that work in both directions; to facilitate extreme trends as well as to deter them. Unfortunately, anti-Muslim bigotry exists, and it's extremely ugly. The mainstream media, especially right-wing outlets like Fox News, Dailywire and other likeminded outlets are playing a significant role in the spread of Islamophobia. News media coverage of Muslims and their religion Islam is one-sided and is depicted in a negative light. This manuscript has analyzed the role that the media plays in Islamophobic hate crimes, focusing solely on Islam and the Muslim community in the United States. The analysis was driven by two questions: *How does media coverage facilitate hate crimes and support perpetrators?* And *how does exposure to violence in the media lead to an increase in violent behavior?* The findings revealed that social media acts as a source of inspiration and makes it easier for perpetrators to associate with terrorist attacks stemming from radical Islamic ideology which is attributed to the entire community. As Muslim minorities are portrayed negatively, this ultimately serves as a justification for hate crimes against Muslims and Islam as their religion.

Islamophobia has been on the rise in the West due to the negative impact media has had on stereotyping Muslims as a safety threat. The increasing violence has consequently shifted the public perception of Islam as an extreme religion that emphasizes violence. The continuing cycle of biased reporting style and victimization of perpetrators will only worsen this issue. As the U.S. society begins to treat hatred with less seriousness, it will sink deeper into the pit of ignorance. Initiatives aimed at addressing this problem need to start with our government and public figures to warn of the risks of rightwing extremism and the reliance of perpetrators on social and electronic media as a safe space for spreading terrorist or extremist content. As indicated earlier in the paper, media coverage can have both positive and negative influence, as it can frame Islamic coverage favorably in an attempt to counter Islamophobia, or it can use expressions such as "Islamic terrorism," "Islamic bombs," and "violent Islam" which contribute to the formation of harmful Islamophobia stereotypes. The fact is that fear of Islam is based on the lack of knowledge of this religion and its teachings. We need continued efforts from politicians and policy makers to ensure that their work and remarks are not divisive or contribute to the alienation of

Muslims in the United States. Thus, factual information and constructive debate in the media will help to stem the growth of negative attitudes among Islamophobes and population in general. It is also important to acknowledge the role media plays in persuading or discouraging the actions of perpetrators, so it is crucial that media outlets are conscious of the messages they put out. The media itself can contribute significantly to fostering common ethical values by adopting an objective approach and not employing sensationalism which gives rise to different phobias and damages peace and stability. Today, as people get much of their information from social media, the largest social media companies should have policies against hate speech on their platforms and take actions to remove Islamophobic content. Openness of religious communities to the media is also necessary for achieving the goals of this process.

Also, in order to give a proper reflection of the multicultural society, democratically run organizations and bodies of ethnic and racial groups should have more access to the governing bodies of the media in the same way as other interests group.

Finally, civil society needs to call on media organizations to cover things properly and not be bigoted or discriminatory on how they're covering the news. Unfair coverage feeds into these ideologies of hate against Islam. Muslims also need to advance a counter-narrative by using social media, blogs, and perhaps community-run media connections, such as Islamic Channels, Islam TV, or local radio, which could present an accurate picture and try to counter the anti-Muslim bias prevalent in the mainstream media. Local mosques and Islamic community centers are good places to seek out community leaders who can point you in the right direction.

CHAPTER 7

ISLAMOPHOBIC GROUPS IN THE UNITED STATES

This study highlights some of the major Islamophobic groups and their activities in the United States in recent years. These groups are actively promoting the deeply mistaken portrayal of Islam and Muslims. The task here is to provide an overview of the main patterns of these Islamophobic groups, their characteristics, leaders and their organizations, their activities, and their sources of funding. Although we have discussed the theoretical perspective of Islamophobic groups in detail in chapter 2, here I would like to mention this perspective briefly again in the context of below-mentioned questions.

Theoretical approach

What type of groups stood behind anti-Islam rhetoric and activity? To what degree were their actions based on ideology and clearly expressed objectives? How was their network and group organized in relation to funding's, and what role their organizations played in spreading hate crime against Muslims and other minorities. These are questions, which will be discussed in this chapter. As discussed in chapter 2, both Mcdevitt and Bennet theory (2002), and Barbara's Perry structured action theory (2001) of 'doing difference' have been widely used to explain why prejudice motivated crimes continue to pervade in most communities. However, neither of these theories adequately explain why some individuals commit hate crimes while others, equally affected by social constructions of 'difference', do not. Most of the scholars do agree that a large proportion of hate crimes committed by perpetrators are motivated by, at least partly by an immature urge to seek thrill, excitement, and public attention.

The following is an example of perpetrators who, after the bombing attack at a religious center, recounted that in addition to scaring immigrants they wanted media attention and publicity that would make people realize that at least someone is doing something for the good of the society.

A White male in his 20s was found guilty by a federal jury for his role in bombing the Dar al-Farooq Islamic Center in Bloomington, Minnesota, on August 5, 2017. Previously, two other defendants pleaded guilty to their roles in the bombing. As proven at trial, during the summer of 2017, the defendant established a terrorist militia group called "The White Rabbits" in Clarence, Illinois. He recruited co-defendants to join the militia, which he outfitted with paramilitary equipment and assault rifles. On August 4 and 5, 2017, they drove a rented pickup truck from Illinois to Bloomington, Minnesota, to bomb the DAF Islamic Center. On August 5, the day of the bombing, several worshipers were gathered in the mosque for morning prayers (USDJ, 2020).

This example above illustrates how general fears of 'difference' combined with thrill and excitement motives become mutually reinforcing factors, propagating a culture of prejudice against certain 'others.' This in turn triggers the hate-motivated behaviors of perpetrators with low self control.

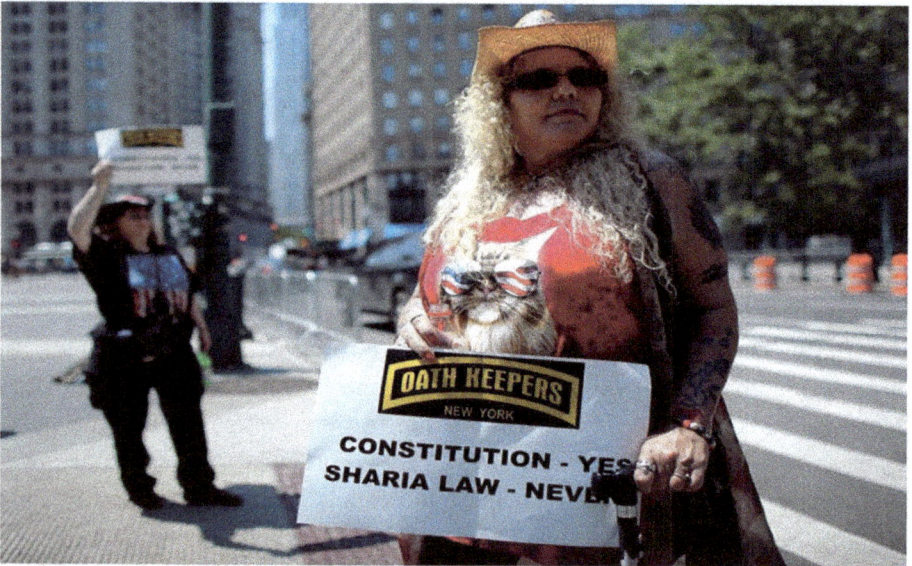

Figure 14: *Trump supporter*
Source: *Kena Betancur/AFP/Getty Images*

Formation of anti-Muslim hate groups

The United States of America is known as the "Land of Opportunity," prompting people from all over the world to emigrate from their homelands, settle in the U.S., and build better lives for themselves and their families. This is the classic American dream, but this dream has grown dim in the presence of racism, prejudice, and hate over the past decades. Many minorities in the U.S. suffer from hate, including Muslims. Anti-Muslim hate groups have been established in order to inflict violence against Muslims, demonize their religion, and exclude them from American society

Hate groups have been a part of history for centuries, all of them having the common characteristic of gathering together and uniting against what they believe to be their worst enemy, which are normally those who are of a different ethnicity or race. "Today, we see some of the same dynamics that led to the rise of hate groups: fear of immigrants, minorities, crime, clashing moral values, and a changing world" (McAndrew, 2017).

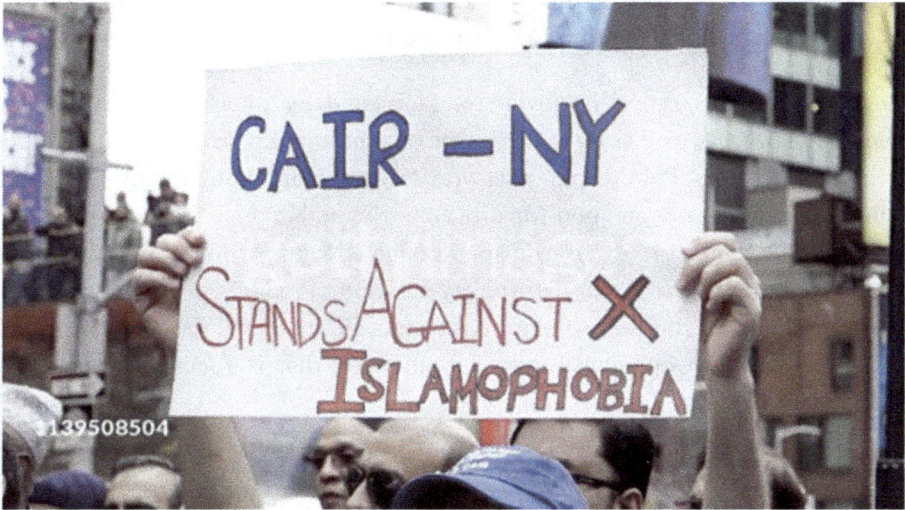

Figure 15: Standing against islamophobia
Source: *Getty Images*

The new concept of Islamophobia has appeared in recent years, and attracted the attention of academics and social scientists in the United States and around the world. The term "Islamophobia" captures a sentiment that might lead to the discrimination of Muslims, which in turn could lead to hate crimes ranging from verbal insults to physical assault and vandalism. The Council on American Islamic Relations (CAIR), whose mission is to enhance understanding of Islam, has stated that Islamophobia has moved from the edge of American social consciousness to the mainstream of its social and political change (CAIR, 2016). Even more recently, particularly after the 2016 general elections, the media report that Islamophobic hate groups and their activities have tripled since Trump's election campaigns at state and local level. Deadly shootings, torched mosques, vandalized homes and businesses, and young people harassed at school have animated the acutely violent post-election years (Fuchs, 2018).

Anti-Muslim hate groups or Islamophobics are a relatively new phenomenon in the U.S. The growing numbers of immigrants from Muslim countries and terrorist attacks committed by Muslim fundamentalists over the last several years' triggered Anti-Muslim feelings in the United States. For example, the hostage situation 1979 during the Iranian Revolution in which Iranian students took over the American embassy and kidnapped dozens of embassy personnel caused a spike in hate crimes against Muslims in the United States and elsewhere. Despite this event's impact on the Muslim community, the bombing of the Twin Towers by Islamic terrorist group, Al Qaeda, on September 11th had the most significant and long-lasting impact on many Muslim-Americans. These events laid the foundation for many hate groups to form and flourish.

Moreover, migration is nowadays facilitated by improved transport and communications as well as by the presence of substantial immigrant communities in the United States. Public opinion is worried about continuing immigration both from Muslim countries and non-Muslim countries and in this climate it is easy for racist or xenophobic groups to gain support and strength. Unfortunately, hate has become a key factor in American society and due to today's political and social discourse the hate groups in America has become more on the rise and prominent. It is detrimental to our constitutional foundation that is focused on equality, liberty, and freedom of expression.

While the Muslim presence continues to grow in the United States, the negative attitude and hate group formation grows too. Hate groups are groups of people who practice and promote violence, hatred, and hostility targeted to a specific race, religion, ethnicity, gender, and any other parts of society. The United States is extremely diverse, and filled with members who believe they are more powerful than others. This perception drives people to spread hate and attract more people that may share the same beliefs as theirs. There is a lot of hatred directed towards Muslims and religion, Islam, in America. It is hard to grasp the idea of people feeling resentful toward a group of people because of their religion and beliefs.

Their characteristics

Some characteristics of hate groups and their members are poverty, corruption, religious conflict, and ethnic strife. These are important to consider because they can show why people join hate groups. For example, a hate group may provide a job for someone in poverty. A corrupt leadership could blackmail or brainwash people into joining. Also, religion is significant because someone may believe they will be "saved" or will go to heaven if they carry out the actions of a certain hate group. Specifically, ethnic strife played a major role in al-Qaeda, the hate group that planned and executed the terrorist attack on the United States on September 11, 2001. Years before the attack, the al-Qaeda leadership stated they were upset with the United States' involvement in the Middle East. These are all ways that hate groups have gained momentum and membership.

Perhaps the most predominant characteristic of hate groups is fear. Their members may feel that their livelihood or way of life is threatened by demographic changes. Offenders may not be motivated by hate, but rather by fear, ignorance or anger (Perry, 2001). This means people are afraid of change and will go to extreme lengths, such as joining and participating in a hate group, to keep their life the way it is. Fear of differences drives hate groups. Fear is also vital to hate groups because that is often what they want to incite.

Hate groups have been a part of our society for many generations and the group of people that run them usually have immense hate of a group they don't consider to be of their stature. In the United States, hate groups and their crimes are directed toward various minorities, such as people of different races, religion, and socioeconomic standing. According to Breen (2012), these groups include like-minded individuals who use prejudice to attain a common goal against an out-group. They come together because of something very simple, and they share a common belief and identity. Breen further argues that people are pulled in through the hate group's messages and their shared characteristics and they feel they are a part of something greater than themselves. Nevertheless, their activities and violent approach only create a larger divide in our society. We cannot move forward to become a more united nation if we do not reduce the amount of hate these groups spread rapidly.

Their anti-Muslim activities

Hate groups have been a part of our society for many generations and are usually run by a group of people who have an immense feeling of hate toward a group they don't consider to be of their stature. In the United States hate groups and their crimes are toward various minorities such as people of different races, different religion, and different socioeconomic standing. Nevertheless, their activities and violent approaches only create a larger divide in our society. We cannot move forward to become a more united nation if we do not try to reduce the amount of hate that is spreading rapidly by these groups.

In recent years the numbers of hate groups focused on Muslims and Islam increased dramatically, jumping after the 2016 presidential elections. Only five groups focused on anti-Islamic beliefs in 2010, but in 2018 around 40 hate groups focus mainly on Muslims, marking one of the largest categories of hate group in the United States (Beirich, 2019). Following the shocking 9/11 attacks, Americans began to view all Muslims as terrorists. Mosques were burned to the ground and Muslims were harassed, threatened, beaten, and even killed in the weeks following the years since the September 11th attacks took place, hate and discrimination against Muslims have not waned. According to the Federal Bureau of Investigation's 2019 hate crimes statistics, Muslims and their religion, Islam, became the second largest target of religious hate incidents following Jews. State-sponsored Islamophobia still exists today as well. The government continues to surveil predominantly Muslim communities in order to monitor their activity, anticipating any possible terrorist attack. Anti-Muslim hate groups are very hostile and claim Muslims have inherently negative traits such as being "irrational, intolerant, and violent," even though they are typically known as a peaceful people. Their Islam faith has also been "depicted as sanctioning pedophilia, coupled with intolerance for homosexuals and women" (Southern Poverty Law Center, 2021).

Organized anti-Muslim hate groups originated after 9/11, exhibit extreme hostility toward Muslims. These groups and their leaders portray those who worship Islam as fundamentally alien and attribute to its followers an inherent set of negative traits. Muslims and their faith is frequently depicted as primitive and intolerant. They have a very closed off mind and believe anyone of a different race and religion are invaders and pose a threat to "their" society (DeAngelis, 2001). The rhetoric from the then candidate Trump made immigration from the Muslim-majority world a core issue of his campaign in 2016, proposing a complete ban on Muslims entering the United States as a "national security measure," but, in reality, it is "a license to discriminate" against vulnerable refugees mostly from Muslim countries who are trying to seek asylum and be reunited with their families. Not only does this type of policy create a negative stigma around refugees and immigrants, but it prevents people who are trying to escape human rights abuses from seeking refuge as well. While some government officials supported the ban, others did not tolerate it. Federal Judge James Robart in Seattle, along with many other judges and justices, came to the aid of these

Muslim refugees and pushed back against the executive order nationwide issuing a ruling that there's no constitutional way to implement an unconstitutional order. In response to Judge Robart's ruling, director of the American Civil Liberties Union (ACLU) Immigrants' Rights Project Omar Jadwat said, "This ruling is another stinging rejection of President Trump's unconstitutional Muslim ban [...] We will keep fighting to permanently dismantle this un-American executive order" (ACLU, 2017). On February 9, 2017, a U.S. appeals court rejected President Trump's attempt to reinstate his ban after Judge Robart's temporary restraining order against the ban. The three-judge panel, suggesting that the ban did not advance national security, and the administration had shown "no evidence" that anyone from the seven nations — Iran, Iraq, Libya, Somalia, Sudan, Syria and Yemen — had committed terrorist acts in the United States.

America, a White man country: Political discourse

While President Trump is no longer in office, anti-Muslim rhetoric is still very present in the U.S. today. According to the Southern Poverty Law Center, Donald Trump's defeat in the 2020 election "left anti-Muslim groups without their top political ally." Trump's absence in office has resulted in a slight decrease in activity from anti-Muslim hate groups, but they are not finished wreaking havoc on the Muslim community. Influential groups, such as ACT for America and the Center for Security Policy (CSP) and some like-minded groups (discussed below), continue to work to develop closer relationships with state and local elected officials in order to continue to push their anti-Muslim rhetoric and agenda. One factor that contributes to the growing amount of Muslim hate is that people who had roles in the office and had publically made negative remarks towards Muslims and their religion Islam. Senior White House officials, including Steve Bannon, Steven Miller, and Kellyanne Conway, are serious anti-Muslim ideologues. Even former National Security advisor, General Michael Flynn has posted tweets on social media saying that the fear of Muslims in America is rational and that Islam is a "malignant cancer." As early as in 2001, Franklin Graham who was an evangelical Christian leader said Islam to be "a very evil and wicked religion that is a direct threat to American democracy (Peek, 2012).

The Muslim-bashing had consequences as we have seen by his selection of appointees in the White House with anti-Muslim sympathies. These individuals and groups represent different hate organizations (discuss in the subsequent sections) and have been responsible for orchestrating the majority of misinformation about Islam and Muslims in the United States today. Their rhetorical strategies consists of relating themselves to a set of symbols and values which are held in high esteem by millions of Americans directed against immigrants, particularly Muslims, and with a threat of reprisal against the political left. The language of politics and the media also contributed to this perception.

According to the Southern Poverty Law Center (SPLC, 2015), the major anti-Muslim groups were successful in meeting and gaining support from the Trump administration while he was still in office. This support from the Republican Party allowed anti-Muslim groups to influence politicians to create policies that align with their hatred for Muslims. When Trump lost the most recent election in 2020, the Biden administration reversed Trump policies influenced by these hate groups like the Muslim ban, the new caps on refugees coming to the United States, and other nativist immigration practices. These were the great steps taken by the Biden administration to remove policies that were aimed at removing and discriminating, particularly the Muslims. It was not right for these hate groups to gain enough power to work alongside with the political leaders to enforce their hatred in the decision-making process by the government. Major anti-Muslim groups were working with Trump administration, which means they shared similar ideologies. SPLS also confirm this view arguing "these groups typically hold conspiratorial view regarding the inherent danger to Americans posed by Muslims in the United States and that Muslims are trying to subvert the rule of law by imposing on Americans their own Islamic legal system, the Sharia Law (SPLC, 2015).

Before the election in November 2016, the Donald Trump presidential campaign promoted extremist ideas that led to the surge in hate groups. A Gallup News survey in 2015 concerning Islamophobia found that prejudice toward Muslim exists among both men and women, young and old, uneducated and educated, with some differences in prejudice levels within different demographic groups. For example, "Men are more likely than women to say they have some or a great deal of prejudice toward Muslims." This survey also reflects American Muslims' likelihood of claiming the Republican Party as their political affiliation. Fifty percent of those who report a great deal of prejudice toward Muslims say they are Republicans, compared with 17 percent of those who identify as Democrats and seven percent as independents. Those who report no prejudice toward Muslims are more likely to be Democrats than Republicans, 39 percent to 23 percent respectively (Gallup, 2015). This survey also concluded that those who only completed a high school level of education were more likely to report feelings of prejudice towards Muslims than those who received any sort of higher education. An explanation behind this is that those who receive more education may be more likely to be tolerant of people's differences. Furthermore, the ideals of political parties may correlate with feelings of Islamophobia as well. Gallup survey also found that those who report prejudice against Muslims are more likely to be Republicans than Democrats. Trump's run for office as a Republican stimulated many Americans, which saw in him a champion of the idea America is fundamentally a White man's country. It's no wonder this idea causes violent behavior in many Trump devotees. Another factor that could contribute to anti-Islamic feelings may include a person's upbringing. The feelings of Islamophobia in one's family may influence them to become Islamophobic, too. If children are exposed to negative opinions of Islam, they can easily be influenced to have these opinions as well.

Angela King, a former supremacist, described her distrustful childhood. She learned racial slurs from her parents, people who she looked up to. Furthermore, while questioning her sexuality in middle school, she was targeted by bullies. She said, "At that point, I decided if I became the bully, no one could do that to me." King said she joined a hate group because she wanted to feel power over others. This also shows that in America, it is common for people who have participated in hate groups to have grown up surrounded by those ideals or have a trauma and personality issue that is seemingly fixed by joining a hate group.

The motivations of individual members are also important to describe. Although their desires may align with the hate group they are in, they may also have personal things they want to achieve. Another, former White-supremacist Tony McAleer, who began a non-profit organization to combat White supremacy and show there is "Life After Hate," has gone into great detail about why he became an extremist. McAleer admitted he grew up with "an unhealthy sense of identity" and by joining a hate group, "I felt power where I felt powerless. I felt a sense of belonging where I felt invisible." This illustrates that the desire to be part of something can draw people to a hate group. McAleer's goal was to find a community and a hate group happened to be one. Then, once you are surrounded by like-minded people, your beliefs become much more extreme and rooted in your identity.

Mosques seen as threatening

Islamophobic groups also typically hold conspiratorial views regarding the inherent danger to America posed by Muslim Americans. Many Americans perceive Islamic practices and sites, such as mosques or community and religious centers, as inherently violent and incompatible with the American way of life. A religious site that received particular attention was a mosque in Manhattan which was proposed to be built two blocks away from Ground Zero in lower Manhattan and was dubbed "the Ground Zero Mosque." One group, *The American Center for Law and Justice,* even sued to prevent the construction of the cultural center, claiming the mosque would be offensive to the victims of 9/11 and their families (U.S. Islamophobia Network Organizations, 2018). The lawsuit was dismissed, and the mosque was ultimately built. However, violent attacks on mosques across the country rose around the time of the so-called Ground Zero Mosque, illustrating the growing anti-Muslim sentiment nationwide.

Gender in Islam: Wearing hijab

Some view wearing a headscarf—the traditional head covering Muslim women wear—and being visibly Muslim as being against American democratic values and by extension contrary to being American.

But why do some Muslims wear the hijab, and what does it signify?

In Muslim communities, women are typically expected to dress modestly from the age of puberty. A hijab is a head covering worn by Muslim women as a symbol of modesty and religious devotion by their own choice. It is not a symbol of male oppression or surrender to family or any authority, as it is often portrayed in the West. The typical and most familiar hijab is a scarf that covers most of, if not all of, the hair. It also covers the neck and falls below the level of the shoulders to cover the upper chest area. Many Muslim women practice hijab in accordance with their religious beliefs, free from discrimination and prejudice. The First and Fourteenth Amendments of the U.S. Constitution bar federal and state governments from making laws or rules that specifically prohibit women from practicing hijab.

A hijab doesn't mean only Muslims can wear it. The wearing of a hijab on the head is a practice that precedes the emergence of Islam and even Judaism. We have found sculptures of ancient, pagan religions that required religious figures to wear head coverings similar to what we know today as the hijab. And as Islam emerged and expanded, women adopted the use of the head covering as an appropriate expression of their own modesty and moral values. But not all Muslim women wear hijab. There is an enormous level of cultural diversity in the Muslim world, and women from African to Asia, and from Europe to the Middle East, all have different ways and codes of conduct to choose for their lifestyle. A Christian woman in Scandinavia probably doesn't dress, think, or live the same way as Christian women in conservative Bolivia or Ethiopia. Besides, other religious traditions also incorporate a veiling or head covering. In some orthodox Jewish communities, married women wear a head covering or a scarf as a sign of their submission to God. Unmarried women and girls are not required to cover their hair, although they may still be expected to dress modestly by covering their legs and arms while in public or in the presence of others. Many Orthodox Christians still adhere to the practice of covering their heads with a scarf or veil when attending church.

Figure 16: *Muslim woman wearing hijab*
Source: *www.pixabay.com*

Figure 17: Christian women wearing hijab
Source: www.iStock.com

Figure 18: Jewish hijab refers to the head covering worn by Jewish women after marriage
Source: Iman Khatib from the Joint List - Credit: Tomer Appelbaum

Images of Muslim women wearing a head covering known as a hijab are not unfamiliar to Western eyes. Different political and social actors widely discussed and commented on social media about this issue. For example, a woman at a Trump campaign in July 2016 in New Hampshire raised the issue of hijab with Donald Trump, who told her he would consider replacing hijab-wearing TSA (Transport Security Administrating) at airports and at borders with retired military veterans.

Following is the brief encounter between the two, which was reported on ABC Television News on July 1, 2016:

> During a question-and-answer session following a trade policy-themed town hall event in Manchester, New Hampshire, audience member Cathie Chevalier asked, "Why aren't we putting our military retirees on that border or in TSA? Get rid of all these hibijabis they wear at TSA?"

> Chevalier, the past state president of the New Hampshire Ladies Auxiliary Veterans of Foreign Wars, was referring to a hijab, the headscarf some Muslim women wear.

> "*I understand,*" *the presumptive Republican presidential nominee responded.*

> Chevalier continued, "*I've seen them myself. We need the veterans back in there to take it. They fought for this country and defended it, they'll still do it.*"

> Trump seemed to affirm the idea, telling her he would consider her suggestion.

> "*You know, and we are looking at that,*" *he said.* "*And we are looking at that. We're looking at a lot of things.*"

Expression against Islamophobia through art

Following is another example of a Muslim woman encountering prejudice and how Muslims and their religion are treated in democratic America today. Through her painting, which she called "Islamic Mural", she is expressing her deep emotions through art. The story is in her own words:

Figure 19: *Iqra Kalsoom Chaudhry with her painting "Islamic Mural"*
Source: *Author*

"My name is Iqra Kalsoom Chaudhry. I am currently working at Deloitte as an Auditor and I have a passion for mental health, art, and seeking knowledge of Islam. With a heavy heart, it took two months to paint this mural. With a lot of tears, a lot of anger, this piece was finally abandoned because art can never be finished. The story behind this piece is that as a part of a national student exchange program in 2017, I was able to study at California State University, Monterey Bay. I was the only visible Muslim on campus and I did not know any other Muslims so I felt like I was not seen and represented. The woman who I painted represents every hijab wearing woman. The word terrorist is plastered on her forehead because that is what we are seen as. Coming out of her hijab are five different figures. The first three are known as "Our Three Winners" and they were massacred in their home by an islamophobe. Their names are Deah, Yusur and Razan. This shooting took place in Chapel Hill, North Carolina and was not seen as a hate crime but as a parking dispute. The next is of a three-year-old baby named Alan Kurdi who was washed onto shore after fleeing Syria. He went on a boat with his parents hoping to seek asylum but lost his life in the process. The third is a Syrian boy named Omar who was in shock

after an explosion hit in Aleppo, Syria and it was heart breaking to see this 5-year-old covered in debris and blood. I remember painting him and his photo was on my laptop as a reference and an art professor passed by and asked me "is that real?" This question was the reason why I continued to paint. It proved to me that Muslims were not represented enough because a professor of a university did not know that Muslims are continuing to get targeted and bombed without reason. All three instances represent how our homes are not even safe for us. Where do we go from here? I painted this to spread awareness and to remind others of these tragic events for not just the Muslim community but also the entire world as members of humanity. I hope that we stay vigilant and protect those around us because a better world starts with better conversations and spreading knowledge and awareness. We have the power to change the narrative and I hope that one day we can feel safe in our homes, in our religious garments, and in our lifestyle regardless of the color of our skin or cultural and religious background".

By using a sequence of five characters, her painting is an example of feelings and emotions that are reflected in this form of art. She created an intense painting in response to an anti hate sentiments against Muslims. The piece began as a form of therapy to soothe the heartbreak, perplexity, and shock that come after her interaction with one of her professors who was unaware of Muslim bigotry. The murder of three innocent Muslim students and the death of children who tried to escape from the war zone areas reflected the artist's personal grief and emotions like love and care, as well as political and social discourse surrounding Islamophobia.

For more information about the figures drawn in the painting – go to the links (see appendices, 3).

Trump stirred up controversy throughout his campaign with controversial comments about Muslims women wearing hijab, and Muslims in general, including vowing to ban Muslims from immigrating to the U.S., until the U.S. could determine and understand this problem of Islamist violence and jihadist intention. He had also suggested monitoring mosques, and said those in the Muslim community aren't reporting the "bad ones" and are protecting them.

Muslims as Jihadist and Sharia law

Many hate groups view Muslims as jihadists who want to undermine American democracy and Western civilization with Islamic despotism, a conspiracy theory known as "civilization jihad." The hate groups allege Muslims are trying to subvert the rule of law by imposing on Americans their own Islamic legal system, Sharia law. These debates—which cite terrorism and extremism to argue that Islam is incompatible with modern society—reinforce stereotypes that the Muslim world is uncivilized. Consistently, anti-Muslim hate groups include members who are White conservative evangelical Christians, fervent supports of the state of Israel, Donald Trump, and far-right Republicans. The goals of each of these groups are also fairly consistent. Each of these groups is often most fearful of the potential implementation of Sharia Law in the United States legal system. In 2010, Act for America helped campaign to add an amendment to the Oklahoma constitution to ban Sharia law from state courts, and in 2017, the group organized a series of 20 protests against implementing Sharia law into the United States legal system (U.S. Islamophobia Network Organizations, 2018).

In a more recent example, the far-right militia groups the Proud Boys have been regularly signal-boosted by and (arguably) communicated with President Trump. The Proud Boys have counter-demonstrated at leftist events, heavily armed and armored, escalating events to violence. Recently, Muslim Americans have become the main target of their vicious acts. White supremacist groups such as these have continued to gain support from Donald Trump, whose own bigoted remarks have been the "green light" in fueling the fire to continuing acts of hatred. In 2015, at a campaign rally, Trump nodded along as a supporter claimed "we have a problem in this country; it's called Muslims." Trump continued nodding, saying, "right," and "we need this question!" as the supporter then asked Trump, "When can we get rid of them [Muslims]?" In response, Trump said "we are going to looking at a lot of different things." In November 2015, on *Morning Joe*, Trump said America needs to "watch and study mosques." A few days later, he indicated he would "certainly implement" a database to track Muslims in the United States. Two days after that, he falsely claimed that "thousands and thousands" of Muslims cheered in New Jersey when the World Trade Center collapsed on September 11, 2001 (Klass, 2019). At his presidential debate on September 29, 2020, Trump responded to a request to denounce White supremacist group, Proud Boys with "stand back and stand by", which was received by the Proud Boys as a positive signal to act. Trump may be unpredictable, but he's been quite consistent when pampering and courting White supremacists. Proud Boys became a household name after a mention at the presidential debate. The Proud Boys are also associated with ACT for America, having attended their 2017 rally "March Against Sharia."

Nationwide anti-Muslim rhetoric gives the message that this kind of behavior towards Muslims is okay. The messages suggest this group is a violent problem, with no evidence or logical reasoning. The White supremacist groups take Trump's discriminatory rhetoric, and put it into action. If a leader of a nation outrightly does not support these groups, there is no possible way these acts of violence will stop.

Anti-Muslim hate spread by Islamophobic groups is a relatively new and consistent phenomenon in the United States, with many appearing in the aftermath of the 9/11 attacks, resulting in a dramatic increase in hate crimes against Muslims since. By far the most dramatic change was the enormous leap in anti-Muslim hate groups. According to the Southern Poverty Law Center, there are over 40 active anti-Muslim hate groups functioning in the United States with chapters in 29 different states, including New York as of 2019 (SPLC, 2019). The 9/11 attackers were al-Qaeda members, which is an Islamic extremist group whose values and viewpoints are not Muslim, although they may identify as such. Since all follow the same religion, they are labeled as "terrorists" and it makes people easy targets. Muslims are then seen as violent individuals and a threat to our society. This even led to a Muslim ban, with some people from Muslim countries refused entry to the United States by President Donald Trump in 2017. The Muslim-bashing had consequences, as we have seen by his selection of appointees in the White House with anti-Muslim sympathies. These individuals and groups represent different hate organizations (discussed in subsequent sessions) and have been responsible for orchestrating the majority of the misinformation about Islam and Muslims in the United States today. The language of politics and the media also contributed to this perception.

The following is the type of rhetoric and comments Americans heard repeatedly after 9/11 attacks: how can be this country not be against Muslims when people we look up to and those who were supposed to educate and guide us, tell us we are to fear Muslims as they are dangerous jihadis and "evil" individuals who want to destroy our country?

Conclusion

The anti-Muslim sentiments are high in the United States. Islamophobic hate groups continue to be a well-funded, tight knit network, with some enjoying mainstream political and social support. They consider America as a White man's country that should be dominated by socioeconomic and political superiority. Anti-Muslim hate continues to run rampant and unchecked on social media platforms. Political Ideological line, such as threat from radical Islam and Sharia law is seen as national security risk and pose a danger to American democracy and values. Influential groups such as ACT for America and the Center for Security Policy (CSP) have developed closer relationships and attracts white supremacist and militia group members from Proud Boys. The Southern Poverty Law Center called these groups as extremist groups that support the Republican Party to influence politicians to create policies that align with their hatred for Muslims.

These groups generally hold that Islam has no values in common with other western cultures, is inferior to the West and is a vicious political ideology rather than a religion. Anti-Islam hate groups portray those who worship Islam as fundamentally alien and attribute to its followers an inherent set of negative traits. Muslims are depicted as irrational and violent, and their faith is frequently depicted as primitive, evil, coupled with intolerance for other religions and women. Wearing the hijab is seen as contrary to American mainstream values such as freedom of expression. Of course, no one should be treated with disrespect for wearing a hijab or discriminated against on the basis of her religious beliefs. Wearing the hijab has always been presented as a symbol of modesty and one of the indications of a woman's moral character. It is ironic that practice of wearing hijab is seen as subjugation of Muslim women's freedom of choice and way of life.

CHAPTER 8

HATE GROUPS LEADERS AND THEIR ORGANIZATIONS

The focus of the present section is on hate group leaders and their organizations, whose ideology is well articulated, which had played a significant role in inciting hate violence against religious minorities, particularly against Muslims and their religion, Islam.

An analysis of groups, which have carried out hate attacks and violence on religious minorities reveals a wide variety of organizational forms and levels, ranging from formal political parties and organizations to individuals and groups, often with ties to right-wing political entities. Their only agenda is hostility towards religious minorities. The goals of these groups are simple. They want to get their message out there and show they are in charge. They use acts of violence to try and prove they are powerful and the one way these anti-Muslim hate groups can carry out their attacks and keep their support rate up is by funneling in money from large charitable foundations and donations.

Nationalism or patriotism

Beginning in 2015, the ugly political discourse of the American election did not end on Election Day. The political discourse on Islamophobia, while highlighting the complexities of national security and terrorism, often appeals to the concept of popular nationalism. In many ways, it has gotten worse and become a national crisis that now challenges American values and identity as a nation. A small group of foundations and wealthy donors serve as the lifeblood of the Islamophobic network in the United States. They provide funding to right-wing think tanks and misinformation experts and individuals who peddle hate and fear of Muslims and Islam in books, films, reports, and websites, thus polluting the national discourse today. Below are some quotations for reflection.

> *"We are the resistance movement, fighting the Muslim invasion of our country and the national traitors assisting them. There 'are only a couple of degrees of separation between anybody on the left and the terrorists - and that includes people in the Democratic Party.' In Unholy Alliance: Radical Islam and the Radical Left, both Muslims and progressives hate America and American values" (David Horowitz,*

leader of the Freedom Center and modern anti-Muslim movement, 2004).

Pat Robertson, President of the American Center for Law and Justice claims:

> *"Islam is demonic and it's a religion of chaos. The government refuses to acknowledge the problem of Islam ... During the Second World War we didn't have any problems saying that Hitler was bad, no problem at all saying the Nazis were monsters ... Now we're fighting a war but we refuse to identify our enemy even though it is in plain sight" (Smith, 2013).*

In the United States, both these organizations (American Center for Law and Justice and Freedom Center and modern anti-Muslim movement) and their leaders are part of the inner core of the Islamophobic network. According to the Council on American-Islamic Relations (CAIR), these groups are categorized as "Inner core", "Outer Core" and "Of Concern". The Inner Core is made up of 37 groups of people that seek to promote prejudice against Islam and Muslims and very obviously portray Islamophobic beliefs. Outer Core hate groups are less explicit. They promote themselves as having different goals, but their work regularly proves to be directed against Muslims and Islam. There are 32 known outer core groups, and they provide funds to White supremacists. The "Of Concern" groups focus less on just Islam, but are still considered an Islamophobic hate group. Each of these are attempting to prevent the success and spread of Islam in the United States (CAIR, 2013). These groups are anti-immigrant activists and seek support for their extreme nationalist views from their interpretations of historic events. History comes to serve as the mythical reasoning for their messages and to legitimatize hatred against Muslims and political opponents as expressed in the above sentiments. Although the ideological points of departure for these two discourses are basically different, the arguments are similar. A civil war will inevitably break out if Muslim immigration and refugees are not halted, and the liberal left did not come to their senses. Such radical perspectives show how desperate these leaders are to legitimize their agenda. After all, America's foundation and traditions are fundamentally based on immigration and immigrants. All Americans, regardless of their religion and ethnicity, respect the American Constitution and live peacefully side-by-side. The problem, of course, is that these leaders idealize an American society founded by European Whites, but reject the principles of egalitarianism enshrined in the American Constitution and the Declaration of Independence.

Figure 20: *Symbol for* Act for America
Source: *www.facebook.com*

One discourse used by the most influential Islamophobic group, Act for America (ACT), is to see themselves as warriors in a clash between Western civilization and Islam. They called for the nationwide "March Against Sharia" to serve as their main recruiting tool, allowing them to remain dominant among other anti-Muslim hate groups. According to an article published by the Anti-Defamation League:

> *"Act purports to advocate for national security and against the threat of radical Islam, but in fact promotes conspiracy theories that Muslims are infiltrating US institutions in order to impose Sharia law. Act fuels irrational fear of Muslims, including 3.3 million Muslims living in the United States, the vast majority of whom are peaceful and law abiding."*

Act for America chapters are located in many states across the U.S. and all hold the same Islamophobic beliefs and goals. The founder, Brigitte Gabriel, was born in Lebanon, but has since moved to America. Due to trauma that stemmed from the Islamic militants in her home country, she has made it her mission to spread her anti-Muslim view. This group was founded in 2007, and is a pro-Trump advocacy group who dedicated themselves to combating the "threat of radical Islam" to the safety of Americans and to democracy. In 2011, on CNN, she claimed that radical Muslims have infiltrated American through "the C.I.A., at the F.B.I., at the Pentagon, at the State Department." In 2014, at the Heritage Foundation forum, she claimed "between 15 and 25 percent" of all Muslims in

99

the world are extremists. She further claimed Sharia or Islamic Law runs contrary to human rights and the U.Ss. Constitution.

In 2017, ACT organized a series of protests in 20 cities across the United States, an event they termed, "The March against Sharia." In these rallies, Brigitte Gabriel has made countless anti-Muslim comments. In one of her statements she said, "If a Muslim who is a practicing Muslim, who believe the word of Quran to the world of Allah, who abides by Islam, who goes to mosque and prays every Friday, who prays five times a day, this practicing Muslim, who believes in the teachings of the Quran, cannot be a loyal citizen to the United States of America" (The Guardian, 2017). The Facebook event pages for these marches were filled with anti-Muslim rhetoric, and the events themselves provided a platform for other forms of bigotry, particularly anti-Semitism. The marches also attracted dozens of members of right-wing extremist groups, including White supremacists who are anti-Muslim and anti-immigration in addition to being dedicated to preserving "White culture," and they found much to like about ACT's mission.

A spokesperson for Vanguard America, a White supremacist group who attended the march in New York City, told the *Washington Post* he doesn't "believe in having Muslims in the United States," and that "their culture is incompatible with ours." In her 2010 book, *They Must be Stopped*, Brigitte Gabriel wrote, "Islam has created and unleashed an uncontrollable wave of hatred and rage on the world, and we must brace ourselves for the consequences. Going forward, we must realize that the portent behind the terrorist attacks is the purest form of what the Prophet Mohammed created. It's not radical Islam. It's what Islam is at its core" (Gabriel, 2010). As these quotations imply, Gabriel does not consider Islam a religion like Judaism or Christianity, but rather a totalitarian political ideology that must be eradicated. Thus, she does not believe Muslims deserve the freedoms of worship and association enshrined in the First Amendment. Rather, they should be stopped because they cannot be loyal citizens of the United States.

Several elected officials have been included and honored at Gabriel's events, including Texas Senator Ted Cruz, Republican Steven King of Iowa, former National Security Advisor Michael Flynn, and New York Republican Peter King, who was given ACT's "Patriot" award in 2010. During the Trump presidency, Gabriel paid a visit to the White House, a report which was first denied by the White House, but a White House official later confirmed Gabriel had visited. The purpose was to make general introductions, which is pretty typical of any new administration, the official said, adding that Gabriel requested the meeting.

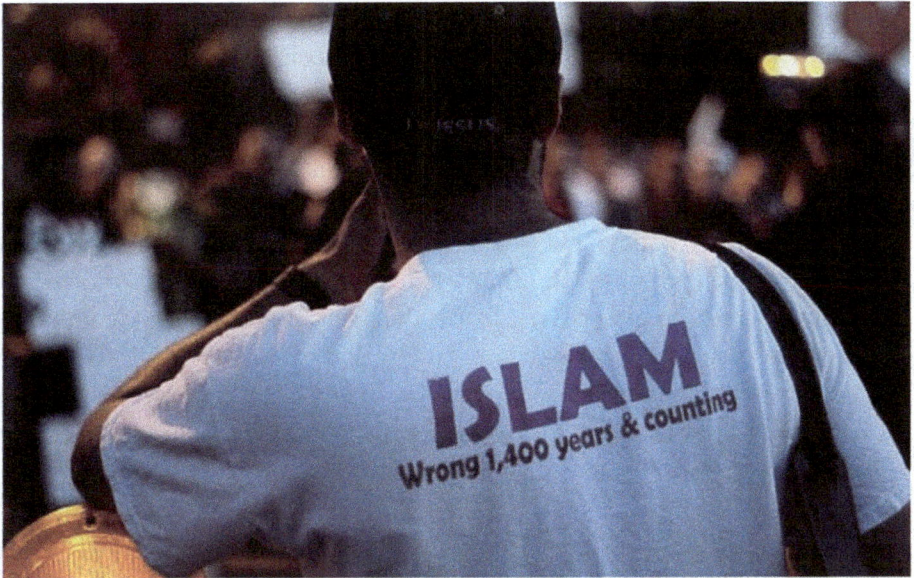

Figure 21: ATC for America
Source: Getty Images

Another example of this bigotry is to ridicule Islam and Muslims by attempting to create an atmosphere of hatred among Americans. Former Trump national security advisor, Michael Flynn, and a board member of ACT, said, "Let us not fear what we know to be true. Let us accept that we were founded upon our Judeo-Christian ideology, built on a moral set of rules and laws. Let's not fear, but instead fight those who want to invade our country and impose Sharia law and radical Islamist views" (*The Guardian*, 2016). In August 2016, Flynn gave a speech at an ACT For America Dallas event. In his speech, he told the audience he doesn't see Islam as a religion and even called it a "cancer" (Tashman, 2016). In its annual report 2019, the Southern Poverty Law Center (SPLC) stated that ACT has stayed true to its mission by working to advance anti-Muslim legislation at the local and federal level while flooding the American public with hate speech demonizing Muslims (Beirich, 2019). In a report published in 2016, Council on American-Islamic Relations (CAIR) examined what it calls the "Islamophobia industry". The report identifies 33 groups, including feminist, Christian, Zionist, and prominent news organizations, which either funded or fostered Islamophobia. According to the report, these anti-Muslim groups had, between 2008 and 2015, access to more than $204m in revenue and helped push for legislation targeting Muslims (CAIR, 2016). Amr Ruiz, a spokesman for CAIR, said, "It is an entire industry of itself. There are people making millions of dollars each year from promoting Islamophobia. They often present themselves as experts on Islamic affairs when they are not". One unique characteristic that most Islamophobic group share is that most of them do not have overtly racist or Islamophobic names, while other hate groups do. While many groups have offensive names such as Aryan Brotherhood, Identity Europa, or Ku Klux Klan, the more popular Islamophobic hate groups have less exciting names such as ACT for America, Center for Security Policy, and Freedom Center. These names don't seem like they belong to hate groups, and instead sound like names for organizations that genuinely wish to help people, and that is the point. By having very comforting names that may appeal to many conservatives, and other Americans affected by 9/11, these groups can bring more people in than if their name was something provoking, such as The Coalition Against Islam. Nevertheless, these groups have a very deep anti-Muslim rhetoric that doesn't change, no matter the name.

Act for America, which I have discussed above, the think tank Center For Security Policy (CSP), and Freedom Center, which I will discuss later in this section, have sought to develop closer relationships with elected officials both at the state and local level. A shift in targets has also taken place recently with the Syrian refugee crisis, as anti-Muslim groups have increasingly directed their fury toward the American refugee program. Refugees are commonly depicted as potential terrorist infiltrators by these two organizations. Michael Flynn served as the National Security Advisor for Donald Trump in 2017. His tenure of just 24 days as National Security Advisor is the shortest in the history of the office.

Numerous Islamophobics and neoconservative individuals, among them Robert Spencer, Frank Gaffney, Steven Emerson, David Yerushalmi, and Daniel Pipes, speak of a "resistance movement" that will wage a war against the liberal left and its fight against the "Islamization of America." These individuals have been responsible for orchestrating most of the misinformation about Islam and Muslims in the United States today. They are actively promoting the deeply mistaken portrayal of Islam, a religion of about 1.8 billion people worldwide, as an inherently violent ideology that seeks domination over the United States and all non-Muslims. Robert Spencer of Jihad Watch and Stop Islamization of America, said in one of his videos that Islam was "the only religion in the world that has a developed doctrine, theology and legal system that mandates violence against unbelievers and mandates that Muslims must wage war in order to establish the hegemony of the Islamic social order all over the world" (Fay, 2017). Frank Gaffney, founder of Center for Security Policy (CSP) makes unsubstantiated claims about imposing Sharia law and the proliferation of "radical mosques" not only through his think tank but also through his Big Peace Blog and beats the drum against the impending threat of Sharia. Although mosques and other places of worship are constitutionally protected houses of worship in America, Gaffney sees them as "Trojan horses" used by Muslims to promote "sedition" (Gaffney, 2011).

Steven Emerson, founder of the Investigative Project on Terrorism, produced a television documentary in 1994 *Jihad in America,* which allegedly "exposed clandestine operations of militant Islamic terrorist groups on American soil." In the documentary, he stood in front of the Twin Towers and warned:

> The survivors of the explosion at the World Trade Center in 1993 are still suffering from the trauma, but as far as everyone else is concerned, all this was a spectacular news event that is over.

> The survivors of the explosion at the World Trade Center in 1993 are still suffering from the trauma, but as far as everyone else is concerned, all this was a spectacular news event that is over.

> Is it indeed over?

> The answer is - apparently not. A network of Muslim extremists is committed to a jihad against America. Their ultimate aim is to establish a Muslim empire (Emerson, 2002).

Emerson added that, "As the activities of Muslim radicals expand in the United States, future attacks seem inevitable. Combating these groups within the boundaries of the Constitution will be the greatest challenge to law enforcement since the war on organized crime." David Yerushalmi, another player who is spreading misinformation about Islam and Muslims, has stated that Muslim civilization is at war with Judeo-Christian civilization and proposed outlawing Islam and deporting Muslims and other "non-Western, non-Christian" people to protect the U.S.'s "national character." In one of his interviews reported in Southern Poverty Law Center (SPLC) on June 26, 2017, he said, "I don't have a problem saying that Western culture and civilization are simply supreme. It's superior to that which is conquered, and I have no problem with saying that Islamic culture is violent, it's misogynist, it's discriminatory and it's backward, and all I have to do is point to the entire Muslim world" (No Author, 2017). Yerushalmi founded the Society of Americans for National Existence (SANE), a hate group that considers Islam the greatest enemy of America.

While groups like ACT for America lobby in cooperation with the government to spread their bigotry, some other hate groups are comprised of vigilantes who undermine the law to enact violence on the Muslim community. We see this approach demonstrated by groups like the White Rabbit Militia Group. The group was founded by Emily Clarke Hari, a male to female transgender woman known as Michael Hari at the time of their arrest. The group was shut down by the FBI in 2020 while Hari was on trial for the bombing of the Dar Al-Farooq Islamic Center in Minneapolis. The White Rabbit Militia Group and similar vigilante groups often fund their activities internally through their own members. Members often gather a collection of weapons and protective equipment. Some of which were acquired illegally. They also receive crowd funding from other similar militia groups. There are videos on YouTube in which Hari is asking for donations from other militia groups. With these funds and weaponry, militia groups can perform violent attacks against the Muslim community in their surrounding area. For instance, The White Rabbit Militia Group uses weaponry to threaten and antagonize groups and business that conflict with their views. The group was also linked to the unsuccessful bombing of an abortion clinic not long before the bombing of the Dar Al-Farooq Islamic Center. The group's most frequent weapons of choice are explosives. Due to its criminal nature, the White Rabbit Militia Group doesn't have a large internet presence. However, they do run a small website, Facebook group, and YouTube page.

Another prominent Islamophobic hate group is the American Freedom Defense Initiative, which may sound like a social justice movement but is believed to be an anti-Islam hate group by the SPLC. One way they have perpetuated hate is by the use of Islamophobic ads in the Washington transit system, as well as drafting them for the New York and San Francisco transit systems. Their most prominent ad from 2012 stated, "In any war between the civilized man and the savage, support the civilized man. Support Israel. Defeat Jihad" (Yan, 2015).

Omnipresent expert in television studios and regular commentator of American mainstream newspapers, Daniel Pipes is the founder of the Middle East Forum and one of the main commentators focused on terrorism and Islam. His mission is promoting American interests through publications, research, media outreach, and public education. He also sponsors the Islamist Watch project, whose goal is to combat the ideas and institutions of nonviolent, radical Islam in the United States and other Western countries. It exposes the far-reaching goals of Islamists, works to reduce their power, and seeks to strengthen moderate Muslims. Daniel Pipes has become increasingly out of touch with the Muslims and their way of life, making more extreme and unfounded observations about Islam in the United States. According to Adib Farha, the author of the article, "Purveyors of Hatred: Muslims Who Fuel Islamophobia", published in the *New York Times* in September 2003, Pipes has enraged many American Muslims by advocating that Muslims in government and military positions be given special attention as security risks and by opining that mosques are "breeding grounds for militants (Farha, 2003). In 2002, Pipes launched his website Campus Watch to monitor professors and academics that deviate from his political ideologies. This website inspired the creation of David Horowitz's "Discover the Networks," established in 2003 to track the political left, and both sites have subsequently shared content. David Horowitz is the founder of Freedom Center mentioned earlier in this section. In addition, Horowitz hosts an annual elite conference "Restoration Weekend" in Palm Beach, Florida, whose participants have included anti-Muslim and Islamophobists Richard Spencer and Frank Gaffney, among other right-wing conservatives such as Steve Bannon, White House chief strategists in the Trump administration and former Republican presidential candidate and former governor of Arkansas, Mike Huckabee. Horowitz's Restoration Weekend has long been a center of right-wing paranoia. These groups and individuals use this opportunity to strengthen their ties with like-minded people—the relative extensive movement of Muslim hate and declared Islamophobics in the United States. Many describe refugees as pioneers in a Muslim army of conquest. This is part of an evil Muslim conspiracy to establish global Islamic rule. In November 2016, these Islamophobes gathered in Florida to discuss a conservative agenda and the Syrian refugee resettlement issue. Some other speakers wondered if President Obama was a secret Muslim. They attacked him and called him a "terror in the White House" who is "at war against Americanism" and "at war against freedom" and who "in every single case sides with the enemy."

Funding Anti-Muslim hate groups: Top funders

Hate organizations and groups on social media need to have some funding to keep their members interested and organize offline gatherings so they can echo their feelings. When these groups need funding, they share their messages with different media outlets like blogs, "the media outlets, in turn, give members of this network the exposure needed to amplify their message, reach larger audiences, drive fundraising numbers, and grow their membership base" (Ali & Clifton, 2011).

One way in which these anti-Muslim hate groups carry out their attacks and keep their support rate up is by funneling in money from large charitable foundations and wealthy donors. They gave millions of dollars to anti-hate groups. They fund right-wing think tanks who promote hate and fear of Muslims and Islam through books, videos, reports, and websites. As a result, an enthusiastic group of anti-Islam grassroots organizations and right-wing religious groups and individuals use the materials as propaganda for their constituency. This is disgusting, because there are people suffering that need that money, while the money goes towards making life miserable for innocent people just because of their background and religion. The Council on American-Islamic Relations (CAIR) says charitable foundations and wealthy donors, mostly mainstream, are directly and indirectly giving millions of dollars to anti-Muslim hate groups. For example, in recent years, the Fidelity-affiliated charitable fund granted more than $330,000 to the Family Research Council, a "research and education organization" in Washington, D.C., whose leader Tony Perkins has called homosexuality "objectively harmful" and advocated for "restraining" the freedoms of Muslims in America. CAIR investigated a money trail and discovered that over one thousand mainstream charities were connected to 39 anti-Muslim groups referred to as the Islamophobia Network. According to the CAIR, the eight top funders contributed $57 million to this network between 2001 and 2012 (CAIR, 2016). These funders include:

- Donors Capital Fund and Donors Trusted: $27, 042,600
- Alan and Hope Winters Family Foundation: $817,060
- Scaife Foundations: $10,475,00
- Russell Berrie Foundation: 3,802,231
- Fairbook Foundation: $1,859,450
- Newton, D. & Rochelle Foundation and Charitable Trust: $1,411,000
- William Rosenwald Family Fund, Middle Road Foundation, and Abstraction Fund: $4,952,979
- Lynde and Harry Bradley Foundation: $6,540,000

Upon further investigation of the Islamophobia Network, it was found that various donors had distributed nearly 125 million dollars to this network between 2014 and 2016. That includes money that was anonymously given through the charitable foundations of wealth management groups, like Fidelity Charitable and Schwab Charitable (Fadel, 2019).

According to a Sludge analysis from 2014 through 2017, four charitable organizations, including Schwab and Fidelity Charitable, have financed more than 30 anti-Muslim hate groups. The biggest recipients groups include the David Horowitz Freedom Center and Frank Gaffney's Center for Security Policy, who received close to $850,000 and $160,000 from Schwab and Fidelity Charitable respectively (Kazeem, 2016). The Council on American-Islamic Relations (CAIR) heavily criticized these organizations for misusing the grants and for spreading misinformation about Islam and fear-mongering about the principles Muslims live by. The work they do has real lasting damage, and they call the groups "the most pernicious" of the anti-Muslim groups identified by Sludge (Gandel, 2019). Likewise, a spokesperson from Southern Poverty Law Center (SPLC) while criticizing these organizations said this is a tragedy that Fidelity is making the decision to follow the wishes of its donors, but we think Fidelity should make the choice not to pass funds to groups that's purpose is to legitimize discrimination and feed violence against the immigrant communities (Kotch, 2019). These organizations, however, rejected the allegations of receiving funds and using it inappropriately. In a statement on January 2018, Schwab Charitable said that it is one of the largest national providers of donor-advised funds and other philanthropic services. Recently, it has expanded their giving priorities in response to the unprecedented natural disasters and the needs of America's most vulnerable citizens. Feeding America, the Red Cross, Planned Parenthood, Salvation Army and Doctors Without Borders were among the most widely supported charities in 2017. It further said that The Internal Revenue Service is an independent public charity that "facilitates grants on behalf of individuals to charitable organizations of their choice. Grants that are recommended by our clients in no way reflect the values or beliefs of Schwab, Schwab Charitable or its management." Schwab further added that it "does not condone hate groups and we take concerns about illegitimate activity by grant recipients seriously" (Schwab Charitable, 2018).

Similarly, Fidelity Charitable also denied these allegations that Fidelity is "bankrolling" anti-immigrant and other groups the funds they received from donors. Fidelity Charitable says it conducts a "robust review" of each grant to make sure, among other things, that charities used those granted funds "solely for proper charitable purposes." Its spokesperson told CBS News in December 2019 that it took the report's findings "very seriously," adding that, "if there are concerning reports identified regarding a specific charity, and Fidelity Charitable determines that grants to an organization are not used exclusively for charitable purposes, Fidelity won't approve grants to that organization. The spokesperson further added, that its charitable fund is "cause-neutral" and that people with concerns about the activities of a charitable organization that its fund's donors support should contact the IRS or state charity regulators, not Fidelity (Gandel, 2019). The Internal Revenue Service (IRS) should have taken notice sooner and acted on these allegations and if the funding is used to advance anti-Sharia legislation or used to stage anti-Muslim rallies or such, these donors and charities who takes tax advantages should be held accountable.

Figure 22: Americans against Muslims
Source: CNN "Anti-Muslim Hate Crimes: Ignorance in Action?"

Other main organizations benefitting from these funds and fueling the Islamophobia network include:

- The Counterterrorism & Security Education and Research Foundation: 120,000
- American Islamic Forum for Democracy; $12,593,745
- Middle East Forum: $12,593,745
- David Horowitz Freedom Center: 10,848,250
- Investigative Project on Terrorism: $1,484,335

- Jihad Watch: $258,250
- Center for Security Policy: $7,050,275
- Society of Americans for National Existence: $477,288
- Clarion Project: $18,508,600
- ACT for America Education: $208,697

These organizations form an often-interconnected group responsible for spreading fear, bigotry, and hate against American Muslims and Islam. This small network of organizations remains very tight-knit, often propagating each other's materials and financially supporting one another. For example, ATC for America, who received $208,697, is the largest anti-Muslim group in the United States. It was discussed in the previous section on *Hate Groups Leaders and Their Organizations*. The Anti-Defamation League (ADL) describes this group as an organization that stokes "irrational fear of Muslims" (no author, Anti-Defamation League, 2017). Recognized as the foremost authority on extremism, the League provides resources, expertise, and training, which enables law enforcement agencies, public officials, community leaders, and technology companies to identify and counter emerging threats. According to the Anti-Defamation League, another way these hate groups collect money to meet the financial needs of their organizations is by collecting dues from their members. These dues can be in the form of a membership fee, monthly fee, or annual fee. Members pay these fees because they feel like their money is going towards the cause and they are brainwashed into thinking their ultimate goal is to achieve that cause, whatever it may be (Anti-Defamation League, 2017).

It is also important to take into consideration that these organizations are collecting money from their members on top of soliciting people and other organizations do it as well. The Internet makes it a lot easier for these hate groups to collect money from individuals worldwide. Without these donations, hate groups would not be able to fully function. According to the Southern Poverty Law Center (SPLC), the money they receive allows them to keep their members engaged, purchase the necessary materials they need to carry out a violent attack, and run continuous campaigns that convince individuals to join their groups. The funds they receive help them to achieve their objectives because it keeps them going (Mark, 2017).

The use of social media by Islamophobic group

Another huge factor in facilitating hate and violence against Muslim Americans is the media. The media has an effect on all members of society. It is therefore important to consider how the media reflects the realities of a society, which is gradually portrayed by ethnic and cultural diversity, and in particular, what images of minorities and racial groups are exposed in the media. The media have given the public a negative image of Muslims. Dr. Idrisa Pandit wrote an article, which highlighted anti-Muslim incidents and crimes and media misrepresentation. She stated:

What often gets overlooked is the impact negative representation of Muslims and Islam in the media has on lives of ordinary Muslims, especially Muslims living in the West. Rise in hate crimes and hate incidents against Muslims, targeted attacks on their places of worship, and attacks on their way of life, contributes to (a) general sense of unsafety and lack of and more recently, a security threat, is an image that is embedded in most media violence, and Muslims as the monolithic "other" is used by many politicians and hate mongers alike to create prejudice and fear (Pandit, 2018).

Dr. Pandit elaborated on many issues in America and the role that media plays in creating these issues. If the media did not spread this feeling of anxiety and idea Muslims are the monolithic "other", the violence and racism most likely could've been avoided or limited at the very least.

Media coverage in America on Islamic hate groups has been severely understated. The media does very little to shine a light on the daily issues Muslim Americans face. Many anti-Muslim crimes receive little to no media coverage, as they are swept under the rug. At the time, negative narratives about Muslims, aided by media outlets like Fox, were reinforced by the government's "war on terror," including the invasions of Afghanistan and Iraq, as well as domestic surveillance programs, biased Countering Violent Extremism programs, and efforts to criminalize Muslims or those perceived to be Muslim due to their faith and appearance. The media shifts stories to change the narrative negatively impacting the Muslim community. Media outlets commonly provide inflammatory headlines and radical click bait to demean Muslims. The media have created a sense that Muslims and terrorism go hand in hand. This has been shown through Internet searches; when searches of news coverage on terrorism increase, so too do searches of news coverage on Muslims. This result reflects that Internet users searching for news on Google in the United States actively search for both in tandem. When there is a crime committed by a member of the Muslim community, the media almost always makes a connection to terrorism. They make the public view the two as a pair. It is apparent that news media have caused the public to view Muslims and terrorism in the same light. This then leads to a drastic increase in Islamophobia among Americans. With this increase in Islamophobia comes an increase in Islamic hate groups.

In a democratic society, there are clear limitations on what governments can do to influence the media, although it is encouraged that media should be more sensitive to community relations, particularly in a multicultural and diverse society. On many social media platforms, there are many groups and organizations throughout these platforms. One particular type of group and organization that seems to have a following of similar feelings of hatred and violence are Islamophobic groups. These Islamophobic hate groups and organizations use these social media platforms to recruit like-minded individuals and encourage these same individuals to take action by all means necessary to protect their shared beliefs. Muslims are portrayed more negatively than other religious groups in the US media, and the average tone of articles about Muslims is considerably more negative compared to other groups. Muslim incidents were more likely to be labeled "terrorism" and linked to other episodes of violence (Kanji, 2018). Leaders of these groups get their followers to facilitate and carry out hate crimes by creating threads, or conversation openers of a certain topic or a non-American group that they feel is "threatening" to their well-being. According to Kianna Gardner, social media also allows something else: "a largely uncensored collection of public opinion and calls to action, including acts of violence, hatred, and bigotry" (Gardner, 2018).

It is a new and disturbing development that makes it possible to gather public support for acts of hatred and violence. Although only a small section of society would condone such hateful actions, it may still constitute a sufficiently large audience for persons who consider carrying out hate and violence against minorities in society. Unfortunately, the hate groups use the media to promote their own agenda. These hate groups have exploited the power of the digital age to recruit new members, many of them young and vulnerable to such overtures, through Facebook, Twitter, YouTube, LinkedIn, Instagram, and other social networking sites. Many people have taken to the Internet in order to spread their ideas through group run websites as well as on social media platforms. People use the Internet to meet other people who think the same way as them. The net allows us to communicate with people from across the world and hate spreads even faster this way. They use propaganda to spread their messages and can easily verbally abuse people through the Internet.

On March 15, 2019, the shooter at two mosques in Christchurch, New Zealand, Brenton Tarrant, uploaded his seventy-four-page manifesto on Facebook before going on the rampage and engaging in his act of terror that would kill fifty-one innocent people. In the manifesto, several anti-immigrant sentiments are expressed, including hate speech against migrants, White supremacist rhetoric, and calls for all non-European immigrants in Europe who are claimed to be "invading his land" to be removed. Journalist Robert Evans described Tarrant's manifesto as "a seventy-four page shitpost," a term referring to low-effort Internet content. It was full of references to other shooters and Internet culture in general, including a particularly horrifying "joke" in which killers are encouraged to get a "high score", meaning a large body count. Evans further says these references are meant to make viewers "feel even more unified as people who 'get' the references and subscribe to the racist views" (Evans).

Effect of media

Social media is a powerful tool that has been shaping the perception of Americans for generations. It is an easy platform for people to spread hate on, like Facebook, Twitter, and Instagram. In August 2021, a Facebook ad was posted that criticized Ilhan Omar and Rashida Tlaib, the United States' first Muslim congresswomen, and linked these women to terrorism. Facebook is constantly working to take these pages down, yet they keep reoccurring under different accounts. Facebook cannot exactly pinpoint who is making these false accounts, but they have been able to confirm that it is the same person or individual making a majority of the pages. Also, the number of White nationalists joining Twitter is growingly rapidly, and a majority of their tweets relate to stories that are out of context and simply racist. When President Trump uses Twitter, the amount of hate crimes increases. President Trump is often known for racist remarks against Muslims and hate speech towards them. On January 13, 2020, Trump tweeted a photo-shopped image of Speaker of the House, Nancy Pelosi, wearing a hijab and Senator Chuck Schumer wearing a turban while standing in front of an Iranian flag. The photo was captioned "the corrupt Dems trying their best to come to the Ayatollah's rescue". It is generally assumed that the post was meant to criticize Democrats for questioning Trump's order to eliminate Iranian general Qasem Soleimani. Regardless of the intent, there is no doubt the image portrays the hijab, turban, and Iranian flag in a ridiculously derogatory way. Sadly, this is not the first time Trump has promoted Islamophobia while in office by using phrases such as "Islam hate us" and "ban Muslims." It is clear Donald Trump has done a great deal to reinforce the tragic idea that Islam poses a threat to the United States.

A recent study published in *Social Science Research Network*, focuses specifically on anti-Muslim hate speech and violence in the Trump era. This study shows that the rise in anti-Muslim hate crimes since Donald Trump's presidential campaign has been concentrated in counties with higher Twitter usage (Weber, 2018). The study further points out that, consistent with a role for social media, Trump's tweets on Islam-related topics are highly correlated with anti-Muslim hate crime and when the president used certain keywords such as "Islam" or "Muslim" in a tweet. It's quite clear that in counties with a higher number of Twitter users, the hate crimes against Muslims are correspondingly higher after the original tweets go out. This study compared Trump's tweets against the FBI's record of hate crimes through 2016.

The media plays a big and dynamic role in how hate crimes are displayed, carried out and facilitated. By using tools such as Campus Watch and Discover the Networks, where compelling headlines influence reader to interact with the site, members of the hate group fill entire chat rooms or comment on social media in order to get people to interact with their pages or view their ideas. Campus Watch is a web-based project of the Middle East Forum, a think tank with its headquarters in Philadelphia, Pennsylvania and was founded by Daniel Pipes mentioned earlier under the section *Hate Groups Leaders and Their Organizations.* According to its website, Campus Watch reviews and critiques Middle East studies in North America with an aim to improving them. Critics of Campus Watch say it is a pro-Israel lobbyist organization involved in harassing, blacklisting, or intimidating scholars critical of Israel. Campus Watch denies these allegations, stating that it "criticizes Middle East studies in North America regardless of whether they address Israel and that Campus Watch supports the freedom of speech of all scholars, regardless of their views and analyses."

The other tool media uses to propagate anti-Muslim hate is a website called Discover Network run by the David Horowitz Freedom Center that focuses on the individuals, groups, and history of groups perceived to be politically left wing. The site was launched in 2004 and its current editor-in-chief is David Horowitz. The website has been criticized for including leftists on the same list as terrorists. Horowitz, who wrote about the alleged connection between these groups in his book *Unholy Alliance,* says, "that groups who despise one another might actually be working closely together, maybe without even knowing it."

By utilizing these approaches, these groups can influence those that interact with them either by influencing their own ideologies or by getting exposure through these actions. With the cyber explosion, individuals took to the Internet to receive their news, as well as, their entertainment. The cyber world became one of the most influential platforms in which one can practice freedom of speech and find people across the country who have the same ideas.

All these individuals and the organizations they represent form an interconnected group responsible for spreading fear, bigotry, and hate against American Muslim and Islam. This small network of organizations remains very tight-knit, often disseminating each other's materials and financially supporting one another. By analyzing statements, verbal exchanges, texts, and other forms of communicative interaction, one can gain insight into how these individuals and their organizations construct their social realities and how they try to influence these realities through their discursive practices. Hate groups continue to exist in American society, and who knows when the next act or terrible violence will be inflicted on innocent people. Their intolerable acts cannot go on as they diminish the well-being and safety of all Americans. Sources of news and media need to further their attention on positive aspects of Muslim faith, and expose and condemn these hateful groups and their vicious actions. The treatment of Muslims has been greatly impacted in recent years. The media and politicians have provided support to hate groups so they could progress and achieve their motives. The prejudice of hate groups and their donors is extremely unfair and inhumane for religious minorities, such as Muslims. It is a problem and needs to be solved for everyone's safety and well-being.

Flags commonly used by hate groups include: Celtic cross, Nazi flag, Confederate battle flag and SS flag

Figure 23: Hate symbols
Source: www.wikipedia.com

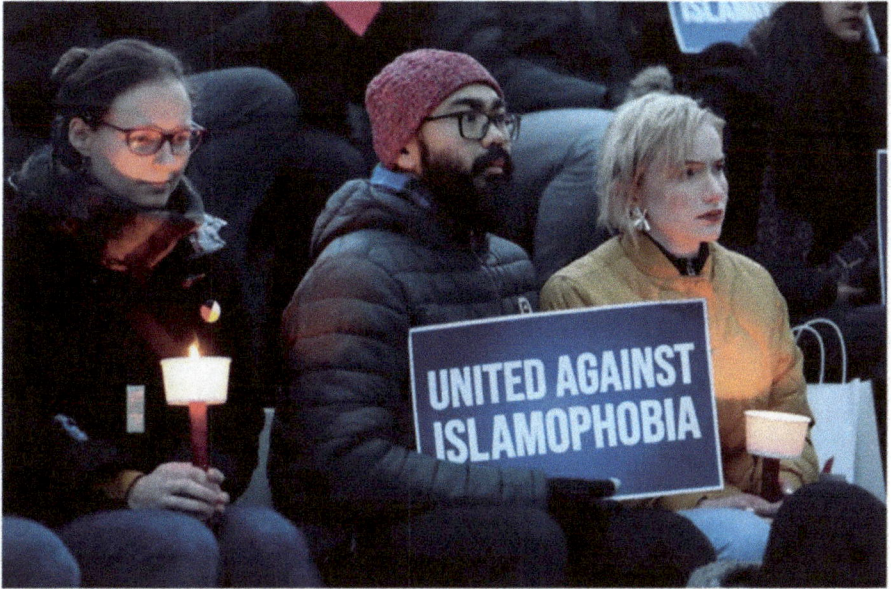

Figure 24: *"United against Islamophobia"*
Source: *Nurphoto Getty Images*

CHAPTER 9

COUNTERING ISLAMOPHOBIA: FEDERAL AND LOCAL EFFORT

Federal Efforts: Monitoring and combatting Islamophobia

On December 9, 2021, the House passed the Combating International Islamophobia Act, which was co-sponsored by Rep. Ilhan Omar (D-Mogadishu). The bill calls upon the president to appoint a "special envoy" to fight "Islamophobia"; this envoy will head up a State Department that will monitor the phenomenon. The creation of the Special Envoy will help policymakers better understand the global problem of anti-Muslim bigotry. It will also establish a comprehensive strategy for establishing U.S. leadership in combatting Islamophobia worldwide. This bill is in the first stage of the legislative process. The committee will consider it before it is passed on to the Senate.

The Council on American-Islamic Relations (CAIR) welcomes the introduction of Islamophobia Bill to establish a special envoy office at the U.S. State Department to monitor and combat international Islamophobia. Nihad Awad, director of the council said on this occasion: "while global Islamophobia, anti-Muslim state policies and hate incidents have increased for the past two decades, the American Muslim community has consistently called for the creation of a special envoy position to monitor and combat this rising tide of hate. Our nation needs better tools to combat Islamophobic state policies and violence. Global Islamophobia is not only a threat to the safety and security of Muslims here and abroad, it is also a threat to international religious freedom and democratic principles" (CAIR, 2021).

Although no new state institutions have been created to combat Islamophobia in recent years, the FBI and the DOJ are increasingly making an effort to connect victims of hate crimes to their respective institutions. Both institutions define hate crime as a criminal offense against a person motivated by an offender against religion, race, and ethnicity and fueled by media (DOJ, 2017; FBI, 2017). The New York State Governor Andrew Cuomo announced on November 20th, 2016 that an "explosion" in hate crimes since the November 8th presidential election has prompted the creation of a special police unit to fight the uptick in New York state. His announcement coincided with an address at Harlem's Abyssinian Baptist Church, where he called for an end to the divisiveness that has gripped the country. "The ugly political discourse of the election did not end on Election Day. In many ways it has gotten worse, turning into a social crisis that now challenges our identity as a state and as a nation and our people," the Governor said in his address. He also announced a toll-free hotline to connect New York residents with the state Division of Human Rights to report any incidents of bias and discrimination and said that New York state's tolerance will lead the way for the rest of the nation to combat hate crimes of all kinds (CNN, 2016).

The Council on American-Islamic Relations (CAIR) has also been very active in combatting Islamophobia. This institution is based in Washington, D.C., and describes itself as America's largest Muslim civil liberties and advocacy organization. It is actively involved in planning rallies and marches and other events nationwide to build awareness about Islam and Muslims in the United States under the agenda "Stop Islamophobia, Defend the Muslim Community." Their first rally was held in February 2016 and those in attendance marched through the Cedar Riverside community, which is home to the nation's largest Muslim community of Somali refugees. CAIR supporters have participated in several protests and demonstrations against anti-Muslim bigotry and other forms of oppression. CAIR (2015) has consistently maintained that, "The mainstreaming of Islamophobia by a number of nation's political and religious leaders has encouraged the latest hate-filled actions of anti-Muslim bigots, now is the time for those leaders who are concerned about traditional American values of religious inclusion and tolerance to speak out against Islamophobia and anti-Muslim hate crime".

On April 24th, 2019, the CAIR hosted a conference about Islamophobia at Metropolitan State University in St. Paul, Minnesota. The conference began with the remarks by Minnesota Democrat Governor Tim Walz, who announced that he would like to open human rights office in his state to fight Islamophobia. He encouraged media to follow Muslim artists, thinkers, writers, and activists, share their work, and portray Muslim voices in the stories they share online.

The CAIR platform also monitors manifestations of Islamophobia in the United States, and collates Civil Rights reports concerning issues such as hate crimes, discrimination, and profiling on an annual basis. It also provides assistance to Muslims in overcoming difficult situations and making complaints against Islamophobic perpetrators. Rallies and protests initiated by CAIR also gripped Atlanta, Austin, Baltimore, Boston, Boise, Chicago, Dallas, Detroit, San Francisco, and other cities across the country throughout 2016 and 2017.

CAIR also called on Senate leadership and the Biden-Harris administration to support the above-mentioned bill, Combating International Islamophobia and making this special envoy position a reality. The bill was passed On December 9, 2021 by a vote of 219 to 212, with all Democrats voting for the bill and all Republicans opposing it, primarily stating that Islamophobia is a loosely defined term that can be used label legitimate criticism of he actions of Muslims throughout the world.

If passed by the Senate and signed by the president, the bill would create an office to monitor and combat Islamophobia in the State Department, similar to the one that exists for anti-Semitism. It would be in place to monitor and combat acts of Islamophobia and Islamophobic incidents in countries around the world.

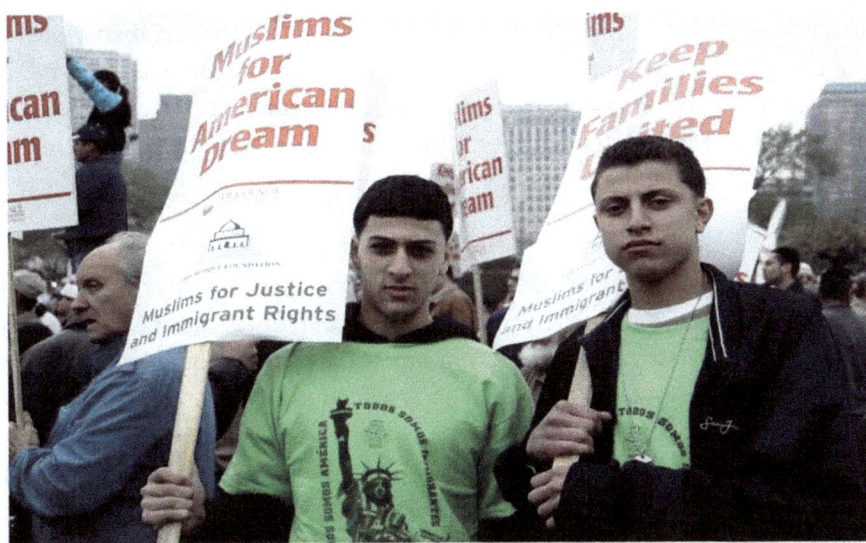

Figure 25: Muslims for Justice and Immigrant Rights
Source: Getty Images

Local efforts

Civil society activism against Islamophobia has also shaped the current affairs regarding Islamophobia, and has been motivated by the growing number of media reports covering Islamophobic hate crimes. For example, in September 2017, the Carter Center convened an international symposium of scholars,

119

journalists, civil society actors, and religious leaders to develop a strategic and sustainable response to Islamophobia in the media and promote positive reporting on Muslim communities. While speaking to the audience, former president Jimmy Carter said, "when we turn a blind eye to discrimination against our Muslim neighbors, we cannot claim to remain true to our American values, and if we tolerate discrimination against those of another faith, we undermine our own cherished religious freedom" (Carter Center, 2017). The Carter Center is a nonprofit, nongovernmental organization founded in 1982 by former U.S. President Jimmy Carter in partnership with Emory University to advance peace and health.

As civil society organization Carter Center recommended the adoption or improvement of public policies against racism, with specific measures to counter Islamophobia. This approach is important because many manifestations of Islamophobia are structural in their nature, in the sense that bigoted patterns against Muslims are embedded in policies, laws and practices of institutional or private bodies. Therefore it is imperative that both at the federal and local level our commitment to human rights and fundamental freedom is preserved and respected. In addition, political leaders should be cautioned on their use of inciting and fiery rhetoric, which fuels hatred and intolerance instead of reinforcing social cohesion and solidary among citizens.

Attacks on a religious minority have no place in civilized American society. Every one of us can make our communities stronger and safer by speaking up against attacks such anti-Islam hate and violence. Our citizens in this country are endangered not only by those who commit such violence, but also by those who fail to condemn it. In 2016, Local Progress and the Young Elected Officials Action Network (YEO Action) joined together to speak out and fight back against anti-Muslim bigotry, and the related xenophobia, racism, and hate that surrounds it. Local Progress is a movement of local elected officials advancing a racial and economic justice agenda through all levels of local government. They are elected leaders who build power with underrepresented communities, share bold ideas and policy among its network, and fight to reshape what is possible in localities all across the country. Even before the campaign began mobilizing officials, the city council would attempt isolated interventions. (In Muncie, Indiana, home state of Trump running mate Mike Pence, for instance, the City Council passed a unanimous resolution promoting religious freedom this past March.) Since the campaign's launch in 2016, these interventions have accelerated rapidly in number as well as kind.

The campaign has so far come up with several policy solutions to reduce Islamophobia. For instance, school districts can write into their bylaws explicit support for Muslim students, and a commitment to hold those who discriminate based on race or religion accountable for their actions. Many school districts have begun to take discrimination more seriously; the American Leaders Against Hate campaign suggests being extra-vigilant about harassment based on religion or skin color, including a formalized tracking system for incidents. Schools can also work anti-bullying and pro-diversity information into their curricula. They can train teachers and guidance counselors to not only know more about Muslim cultures but also to know how to spot bias within themselves and their students, and how to deal with it.

To fight against Islamophobia, more than 500 elected officials signed on to an open letter in 2016 condemning bigotry and pledging to support Muslims and other minorities who have come under attack in their communities. A branch of Local Progress office in Washington, DC published the letter on September 29, 2016, in the face of an alarming spike of an anti-Muslim hate.

Commenting on this open letter, the U.S. Representative Keith Ellison (D-MN) said:

> *"As the first Muslim member of Congress and the chair of the Congressional Progressive Caucus, I am so proud and appreciative of the hundreds of local elected officials from around the country who have stood up against hatred and anti-Muslim bigotry." He further said that "Local Progress and the Young Elected Officials Network Action are doing essential work organizing leaders from cities and states around the country, and their work on this campaign will strengthen our country and help protect the Constitutional rights of all Americans and immigrants to practice their faith and live dignified lives in our great country."*

Commenting on the letter, Meshea Poore, YEO Managing Director expressed his views:

> *"We cannot sit idly by and watch as our friends and neighbors are vilified and attacked because of their religious beliefs, attire, or race,"* it is clear that hatred and bigotry goes against the fundamental rights and freedoms guaranteed in our country."*

The letter and the reaction to it marks the start of a coordinated campaign in cities across the country to push back on increasing attacks on Muslims, which have reached levels unseen since September 11, 2001. To escalate the cause further, the New York City Council Progressive Caucus also released an open letter in September 2016 condemning bigotry, Islamaphobia and pledging to support Muslim and immigrant communities who have come under attack. Signers vowed to take action to ensure that the Constitutional rights of all members of their districts are protected and that all residents are welcomed as full members of our community. The letter was signed by mayors, and state and local legislators including Caucus members and a total of 33 NYC Council Members.

With these considerations, the New York City Council passed a resolution pledging to combat hatred and anti-Muslim bigotry. The resolution was sponsored by Council Member Daneek Miller, sole Muslim representative in the Council, Council Member Carlos Menchaca, Chair of the Committee on Immigration, and Council Member Brad Lander, Board Member of Local Progress. On the occasion the Council Member Daneek Miller said:

> *"New York was founded by people seeking religious freedom and its elected body has an obligation to uphold those ideals. With the increased attacks on Muslims and Islamophobia rising across the country, it is important we continue to stand together against hate, and I am proud to have introduce Resolution 1230 declaring support for Muslim communities across the City. The New York City Council has recognized Muslims who have given back to their communities and ensured youth practicing our faith do not have to choose between going to Mosque and missing school during the Eid holidays. This is progress we can all be proud continued support (New York City Council, 2016).*

Since these local activities to combat Islamophobia, cities around the country passed resolutions pledging to combat hatred and anti-Muslim bigotry. Currently there are 45 jurisdictions condemning Islamophobia that are introduced in recent years at both city council and school board levels (see appendices for details).

Other pro-Islamic efforts against hate groups: "I am a Muslim too"

I participated in a direct observation of a protest rally in Times Square on February 19, 2017. The demonstrators gathered to denounce what they see as threats and pressure aimed at Muslim communities. The rally "Today, I Am A Muslim Too" took over Times Square, known as the Crossroads of the World. Thousands of participants of various ethnicities and religious faiths proclaimed "I Am A Muslim Too" with a huge American flag serving as the rally's backdrop. "What's happening in our country requires that people take a moral, an ethical stand for people who can't stand for themselves," said one protester. Some protesters chanted, "This is what democracy looks like," and "We are here unified because of unity with the Muslims." Others held placards of a Muslim woman draped in a headscarf depicting the American flag. One woman said, "I won't speak too harshly of him today, but want to thank him for bringing us together".

Another protester told me, "I came here because I want peace and dignity for everyone, regardless of their race, ethnicity and background." He further said, "We're all humans and we all share the same world and deserve respect for all religions and a place to be happy and healthy." One protester, who was a Jew, told me, "Whenever my Muslim brothers and sisters are demonized and victimized by hate crimes and violence, I feel like saying that "Today, I am a Muslim too." The I Am A Muslim Too rally was designed to support Muslim Americans and organized by several groups, including the non-profit organization Foundation for Ethnic Understanding (Toppo, 2017).

Mayor Bill de Blasio was among the speakers at the rally. This is what he said addressing the rally:

> *"Here's the message I want to give as mayor of this city to everyone who's here. de Blasio said. "And to everybody, this is your country too. This is your country, too. And think about the origins of this country—a country founded by people fleeing religious persecution. A country founded to respect all faiths and all beliefs. This is who we are as Americans, and this must be protected."*

Figure 26: *Americans carrying pro-Muslim posters*
Source: *CNN – Pro-Muslim rally in New York, February 19, 2017*

The protesters—many of them hoisting placards featuring a woman in an American flag hijab with the slogan "we the people are greater than fear"— gathered at one of the world's most famous public places, Times Square, to denounce what they see as threats and pressure aimed at Muslim communities. The rally, called, Today I am a Muslim too," was billed on social media as a day of solidarity with Muslims in reaction to the vicious attacks by President Donald Trump, who has made numerous critical remarks about Muslims.

The rally was hosted by musician Russell Simmons, who told those at the rally to focus on how Trump, his onetime friend, had unified the people in attendance. Religious leaders from over 50 organizations took part in the rally, including Rabbi Marc Schneier, president of the non-profit organization Foundation for Ethnic Understanding (FFEU), and Imam Shamsi Ali of the Jamaica Muslim Center. Russell Simmons and Trump were once close friends but had a falling out in 2015 after Trump announced his candidacy for president.

View the flyer below.

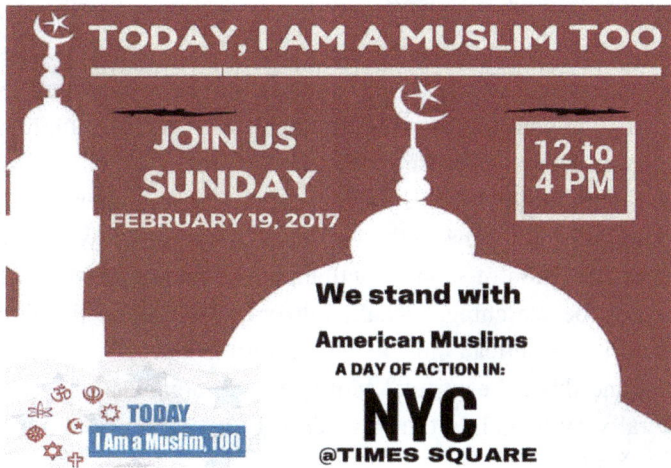

Figure 27: Invitation to join the rally: Today, I am a Muslim Too
Source: Interfaithcenter.org

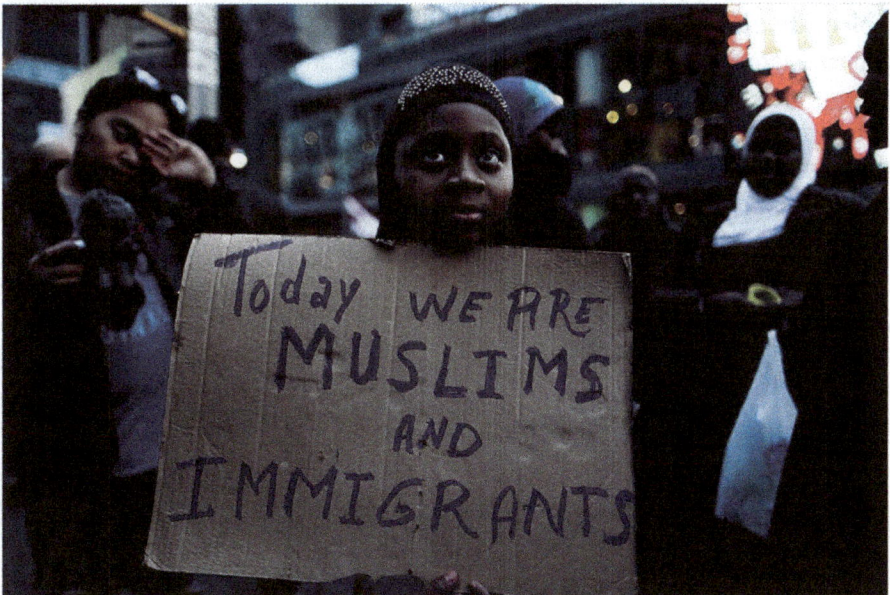

People take part in a rally dubbed 'I am Muslim too' in a show of solidarity with American Muslims at Times Square, New York   (Eduardo Munoz Alvarez/Getty Images)

Figure 28: People take part in a rally dubbed "I am a Muslim too" in a show of solidarity
with American Muslims
Source: Getty Images

I also participated in a Battery Park rally in New York on January 29, 2017, as a participant observer. In this rally, more than 10,000 protesters chanted, "No hate, no fear, we are all Muslims, immigrants are welcome here." New York Mayor Bill de Blasio who was also present there, said, "One example we have to remind Americans is the 900 Muslim officers that protect the city of New York." Khalil Ahmed of Smithtown and his wife both came to Battery Park; they are Pakistani immigrants and came to the United States some 25 years ago. He told me, "I was a combination of sadness and anger. To be honest, this won't be the last time we will be marching." Khalil felt optimistic about the rally and the message behind it. "American citizens will not go to asleep," he said. "This is a positive force, and this is beautiful." Multiple local organizations sponsored the Battery Park rally by including the New York Immigration Coalition and Make the Road New York.

Movement to End Racism and Islamophobia (MERI) is a network of North Carolina organizations with a mission to end racism and Islamophobia. In 2016, MERI members facilitated presentations and workshops on Islamophobia throughout North Carolina and other states. These events were organized to explore the roots of Islamophobia and are specially oriented towards the fight against Islamophobia and protecting Muslims. Finally, there are several smaller groups, mostly Muslim associations and faith-based organizations, which took part in fighting this hateful prejudice, such as Muslims for Social Justice, Foundation for Ethnic Understanding and, Chanukah Action Against Islamophobia and Racism, which is a Jewish Voice for Peace group. These organizations reject policies that criminalize immigrants, refuse refugees fleeing violence, and discriminate against Muslims and Islam. Terming such xenophobia and hatred a "dangerous trend," Rabbi Marc Schneider, president of the Foundation for Ethnic Understanding, which helped organize the anti-Islamophobic rally, "I am a Muslim too", said Jews fleeing Nazi Germany faced barriers similar to those Muslims face today. "Thousands of Jews who wanted to come to these blessed shores were shut out. Never again," he said. "The Muslim community is our greatest ally in fighting terrorism and extreme fundamentalism" (Newsday, 2017).

Some liberal politicians in the United States who have criticized Israel are condemning the anti-Semitic violence but also suggesting that there is a concurrent rise in Islamophobia since violence renewed between Israel and Hamas recently. Senator Bernie Sanders (I-Vt.), an outspoken critic of Israel, condemned "disturbing anti-Semitic attacks and a troubling rise in Islamophobia" in the country. "We've recently seen disturbing antisemitic attacks and a troubling rise in Islamophobia. If you are committed to a future of equality and peaceful coexistence, please stand united against anyone who promotes hatred of any kind," Sanders tweeted on May 29, 2021. Republican Rashida Tlaib (D-Mich.) shared Sanders' tweet with a quote from Martin Luther King Jr. and said, "We won't be free if we come from a place of hate, violence, and racism."

Facebook CEO Mark Zuckerberg said White supremacists and neo-Nazis are a "disgrace," and Facebook has already taken down "any post that promotes or celebrates hate crimes or acts of terrorism. " He said Facebook's policies have long banned violent threats and hate speech, but the platform has sometimes struggled with enforcement (Bell, 2017). Twitter also reacted following the Charlottesville terror attack. In an internal email, Twitter CEO Jack Dorsey detailed more aggressive policies, including treating hateful imagery and hate symbols on Twitter as "sensitive media." Like adult content and graphic violence, the content will be blurred and users will need to manually opt in to view, she explained (O'Brian, 2017). Also YouTube, and its owner Google, promised to do more to identify and remove hateful content on their platform. In Google in Europe, Kent Walker states, "terrorism is an attack on open societies, and addressing the threat posed by violence and hate is a critical challenge for us all. Google and YouTube are committed to being part of the solution. We are working with government, law enforcement and civil society groups to tackle the problem of violent extremism online. There should be no place for hate or terrorist content on our services" (2017).

YouTube also said it intends to intensify the enforcement of its existing policies regarding channels that repeatedly violate the updated hate speech policies. YouTube will suspend channels that violate the hate speech policies from the YouTube partner program, effectively removing their ability to run ads on their own content and ban them from using other monetization features.

INTERVIEWS WITH TWO MUSLIMS

Nayyar Imam

Nayyar Imam, a religious Muslim scholar and an interfaith activist has a good record of community service. Through schools, place of worships, and non-profit organizations, he dedicated his commitment to help children, senior citizens, general public and common citizen. He devoted his time and energy for the betterment of everyone. The community where he lives is still reaping the benefits of his service. Imam is concerned about Islamophobic sentiments and warned that such profiling of entire peoples and communities by religion or ethnicity has grave antecedents. Seventy-five years ago, he said, this led to the Holocaust. We need to pursue policies that respect the dignity and rights of all people, regardless of race, religion, immigration status, or country of origin. Imam gave examples of good practice countering Islamophobia. For example, he argues that interfaith projects on Long Island highlighted conviviality and cultural compatibility between Muslims and non-Muslims. It is also worth mentioning that media outlets such as Facebook and Twitter have struggled with how to handle hate groups on their platforms. After the Charlottesville incident in Virginia in 2017,

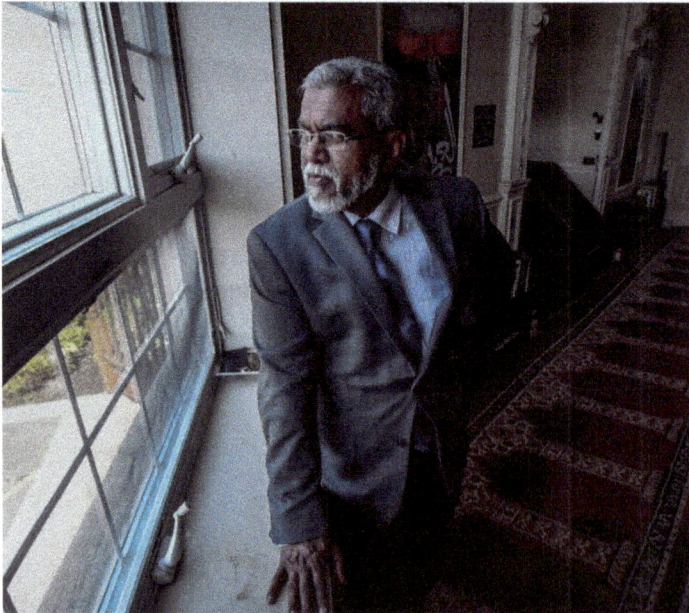

Figure 29: Nayyar Imam, religious scholar and interfaith activist
Source: *Author*

To further shed light on the findings that emerged through a review of Islamophobic context, Nayyar Imam, was interviewed to gain his insight into strategies that could be adopted to counter Islamophobia and the role of interfaith dialogue in changing the narrative about Muslims in the West. Imam explained that the Islamophobic perpetrators are engaging in acts of passion due to racial and religious scapegoating. He was of the view that, particularly after the 2016 presidential election, things have been more fearful for Muslims in the United States. Some of the media perpetuates highly Islamophobic views, which are mobilizing far-right people to attack Muslims. Thus, the Imam opined that the mainstream media should have more balanced and positive coverage of religious and ethnic minorities as a way of promoting peace and harmony in our society.

Iman also welcomes the introduction of Congresswomen, Ilhan Omar, Combating International Islamophobia Bill passed in the Congress in October 2021. It is vitally important that the United States establish a Special Envoy to combat the menace of Islamophobia," he said. "We should stand in solidarity with Muslim victims of hatred and bigotry and I urge members of our community as well as other Americans to pass this important bill when it is introduced in the Senate."

The following are some of the questions I asked Imam regarding the issue of Islamophobia:

> *"Do you consider Islamophobia a major challenge in the United States today? There are periodic assaults on mosques and other forms of prejudice against the Muslims that are investigated by government agencies. Does that mean that there is systematic Islamophobia in America?"*

He stated that he believes Islamophobia is systematic in the United States. There has been surge in Islamophobic incidents in the United States since the election of Donald Trump in 2016. We have some reporting from the Southern Poverty Law Center (SPLC), a nonprofit organization that supports Muslims and advocates against Islamophobia, which indicates that the Trump rise has resulted in a backlash against Muslims and other minorities. As a response, American Muslims have sought out assistance from the Department of Justice (DOJ), Federal Bureau of Investigation (FBI), and Center for American-Islamic Council (CAIR) seeking to advance equality and racial justice. This offers an opportunity for the Muslim Americans to combat Islamophobia both within the Muslim community and from outside of the Muslim community. Imam stated, "I also believe that Islamic religious institutions and Muslim rights organizations such as U.S. Council of Muslim Organizations (USCMO), Islamic Society of North America, (ISNA), Muslim Public Affairs Council (MPAC) and Islamic Circle of North America (ICNA) are among the largest at the national level and have a major responsibility to educate the public about Islam as a faith and the contributions of Muslims to their societies. Since I have worked with some of these organizations, I know that they work hard to raise awareness among Americans by educating and advocating for relevant policies on the state and federal levels. I also believe that we should reach out to the elected officials to express our concern about the Muslim community who is facing today the rise of Islamophobia and discrimination. This menace is not going to go away unless we fight it together at local level as well as federal level. At an individual level, I think it is also imperative that we should reach out to interfaith community and public leaders to discuss intercultural relations, but this is not enough, we need to do more.

"What do you think about the role of the media in portraying an accurate image of Islam and Muslims in the United States?"

Imam answered, "Hateful and racist language, against Muslims or other religious or minority groups, has no place in our democracy or any arena in American society. We must always speak out and stand up against it and seek to unite communities. It is unfortunate that Muslims tend to be negatively framed in media, while Islam is dominantly portrayed as a violent and aggressive religion. Look at how media portrays white mass shooters and Muslim mass shooters. If you look at white shooters who are mass shooters typically in the United States, that is a form of domestic violence and perpetrators tend to have mental issues. But if you brought forward somebody with a brown face, then they are labeled as a Muslim terrorist. It is really the label that they're putting on these people and making them look bad." Imam continued that the media's depiction of Islam leads to a general climate of mistrust and hatred against Muslims and their religion Islam. Media should be acting as a watchdog of what society is getting itself into. Imam also highlighted the importance of holding media accountable when their coverage disproportionately focuses on Muslim violence, inaccurately depicting Islam as a violent religion. People need to call on media organizations and their network to cover things objectively and not be bigoted or discriminatory on how they're covering the news. He said, "I believe that unfair coverage feeds into these ideologies of hate against Muslims and other minorities. But I also think there are reasons to be optimistic about the future of this situation. Those of us who have struggled to bring greater understanding and respect for one another will not allow hate to triumph. We will continue to stand strong, with love and tolerance as our tools, resolute in our constant pursuit of justice in all its forms." Imam continued further and said, "In addition to interfaith dialogue and social networking, Muslim institutions and their academics have to work actively to change the media's negative narrative on Islam. The work of Center for American-Islamic Council (CAIR) with whom I also worked as well as other institutions and organizations mentioned above is one good example of this activity."

> *"What did you do as a community leader and a Chaplain to combat Islamophobia in the United States? What is the best counter measures against Islomphobia you would suggest?"*

"We must be vocal in our positive affirmation of the values that represent our communities. Islamophobia must be whole-heartedly condemned in any circumstance. I personally detest prejudice and hate, and I commit myself to protecting the rights of everyone to live in security and peace. For several years I have visited local schools to explain Islam and its misconceptions. I have also invited school children to local mosques to introduce them about our religion so they can understand that religion Islam teaches peace and love. Likewise, I appreciate the important efforts taken by numerous school districts to incorporate workshops, teacher and administrative training programs focus specifically on Islamophobia. I have participated in some of these meetings and talked about Islam and are our responsibilities of being an educator. I have observed an interest by school districts on this front, as well as their interest in connecting this to curriculum review. I think it is positive to create safe and inclusive space in schools for Muslims and educators. This will bring a clearer and better understanding of Islam and it's teaching, and we should continue our efforts in this regard. I am also very supportive of intercommunal and interfaith relationship. I believe in coalition building among civil society organizations and interfaith partners with focus on city councils and mayoral offices to adopt legislations as they have recently done in New York City and some other cities, vowing to support Muslim and immigrant communities who have come under Islamophobic hate attacks. These initiatives are a breath of fresh air that must be supported and encouraged.

In the Suffolk police academy, I have given lectures about Islam and Muslim community. I believe that frank and honest dialogues about religions, including their differences and similarities, strengthen interfaith relationships. In interfaith meetings in our community, I told my Jewish and Christian participants, "Let's talk about the hate that surrounds us, let's talk about the challenges we face, lets stand together and work towards peace and harmonious relationship among us, lets work together and build on peace and harmonious bond." In these meetings, I distributed copies of Quran and other Islamic literature to religious leaders of other faith, which they have always appreciated. I think these local steps are very important to raise awareness among Americans of different faith to understand Muslims and that how Islam promotes the concept of love and peace, which advocates tolerance. It is through these initiatives that the Muslim communities can more proactive citizens engaging with society and promulgate Islam and its true understandings.

The last concern, I think is the media and the Internet where Islamophobia has had a long and influential presence in spreading bigotry and anti-Islamic hate without end in sight. I believe that the openness of religious communities to the media and their resolve in preventing deviant versions is necessary for achieving the goals of this process."

Moez Ahmed

Another interview was also held with Moez Ahmed, a Pakistani-born Muslim who was secretary of the Muslim Students Association at Stony Brook University. He discussed how Islamophobia surged after Donald Trump made an Islamophobic remark, highlighting that "Trump phenomenon is recent, but the media has been circulating these narratives for a while." He further shared, "Our problem is how to reach an audience outside of interfaith meetings and to convey to them that Islam is a peaceful religion and that the Muslims in the United States are peace loving and law abiding citizens. The people who come to the interfaith meetings and events usually understand the issue and have respect for each other's religion. Misinformation about Islam was a factor in influencing people to develop Islamophobic views, and the media has created a perception that radicalism in Islam is the norm rather than the exception." He further pointed out that NGOs must address Islamophobia by establishing forums in which active opinion makers, religious leaders, and theologians take part, and their messages against Islamophobia must be spread on social media and networks. Ahmed emphasized that the media needs to transform its overall philosophy whereby it understands the pervasive problem of Islamophobia in its representation, including its lack of objective representation of Islam. Ahmed also emphasized the importance of educating younger people about different faiths and cultures. In his view, "it is important for people of all faiths, and of no faith, to educate children about respecting people of various religions, and teaching them to respect people who may be different from them. Education is key to stopping hate crimes against Muslims and other vulnerable groups, and with so many ugly ideas gaining traction, it's more important than ever."

Other Muslims' views

Other Muslims were contacted to share their views and thoughts on the topic. A sample of what they said about Trump and his Islamophobic rhetoric is presented below.

> *"A lot of us Muslims, we don't feel safe here anymore. Islamophobic behavior is bad for Muslims."* – Muslim man in 20s.

> *"Donald Trump is a racist, OK? I'm a Muslim woman. He's not for us. He's nationalist egocentric and is dangerous for the country this is what I believe."* – Muslim woman in 30s

> *"People think all Muslims are the same," "Fear and prejudice about Muslims are based on ignorance about Islam and Muslim cultures."*- A Muslim teacher of Middle Eastern Studies. He continued:

> *"Another factor is the resurgence of American nationalism. The "othering" of Muslims since 9/11 has had a long-term impact on the lives of Muslim Americans and their sense of belonging and inclusion in the fabric of American society."*

Several other Muslim respondents discussed their experiences with the media portrayal of Muslims, from being called a bomb threat to terrorist, or Osama lover, but due to the limitations of time and space, these interviews cannot be discussed further.

U.S. Muslims face serious challenge of Islamophobic hate, but they are also increasingly motivated to confront them. Their efforts both at a national level as well as local level shows how minority and religious groups in America work to secure their collective interests and continue the process of building an inclusive democratic society.

CHAPTER 10

ISLAM AND THE FOUNDERS:

AN ENLIGHTENED APPROACH

Thomas Jefferson and the Quran

Sheharyar Ali, a Muslim Deputy County Attorney from New York, mentioned earlier, seeks to understand the role of Islam in American constitutional history. At a time when most Americans knew nothing or little about Islam, Thomas Jefferson, one of the Founding Fathers and third president of the United States, imagined Muslims as future citizens of his new nation. His engagement with the faith began with the purchase of a Quran eleven years before he wrote the Declaration of Independence. Jefferson's Quran survives still in the Library of Congress, Washington, DC, serving as a symbol of his and early America's complex relationship with Islam and its believers. That relationship remains of vital importance even to this day, says Ali. He wonders how Islam fits into eighteenth-century American's model of religious freedom and utilized Thomas Jefferson in his arguments. Ali says that religious suspicion and bigotry were common during the American founding and after, as it is today, arguing that the rights of Muslims have been a feature of the nation's political and social discourse for centuries. Though Jefferson, along with other believers, was a harsh critic of Islam as a religion and called it anti-science and anti-religion, he also was a staunch advocate of religious freedom and diversity even for those falling outside the prevailing Protestant mainstream, including Catholics, Jews, and Muslims.

In 1783, the year of the nation's official independence from Great Britain, another founder, George Washington, had views about religious diversity that were reflected in a letter to his friend seeking a carpenter and bricklayer to help at his Virginia home. He explained the workers "beliefs—or lack thereof—mattered not at all. If they are good workmen, they may be of Asia, Africa, or Europe. They may be Mahometans (Muslims), Jews or Christian of any Sect, or they may be Atheists". Clearly, Muslims were part of Washington's understanding of religious diversity that existed among immigrant Americans who were mostly from Europe. But he would not have actually expected any Muslim applicants for the work. At the time, Muslims were referred to as "Turks" or "Mahometans," and while an estimated 20 percent of enslaved Africans were Muslim, many Americans at the time didn't acknowledge that Muslims existed in America, according to several historians. George Washington did so, however, not for the sake of actual Muslims, because none were known at the time to live in America. Instead, he, along with Thomas Jefferson, James Madison, and others, defended Muslim rights for the sake of "imagined Muslims," the term introduced for the future possible citizens of the nation. Indeed, this defense of imagined Muslims or future Muslims would also create political and social opportunity to consider the rights of other minorities whose numbers in America, though small, were quite real, namely Jews and Catholics who migrated from Europe to seek religious freedom and better opportunity in the new nation.

Founders views about Muslims

Immigration to the United States in the 18th and 19th century from Europe changed the American religious landscape and sparked anti-immigration responses. Irish immigration led to anti-Catholic sentiment and Jewish immigration to anti-Semitism. Anti-Irish sentiment during and after the new nation was born manifested themselves through the stereotyping of the Irish as violent and criminal. Irish laborers were singled out in particular for rough treatment by the locals and even their neighbors. Farms employing Irish labor were subject to violent threats and harassment. Jews faced the same threat and hatred from the mainstream American Protestants. Anti-Semitism was at its peak as the Jewish population, although very small, felt vulnerable as Americans debated their loyalty and belonging. Hundreds of years of prejudice, hatred, and violence toward Jews influenced these debates.

In 1783, George Washington wrote to recent Irish Catholic immigrants in New York City. The American Catholic minority of roughly twenty-five thousand then had few legal protections in any state and, because of their faith, no right to hold political office in New York. Washington insisted, "the bosom of America" was "open to receive the oppressed and the persecuted of all Nations and Religions; whom we shall welcome to a participation of all our rights and privileges." He would also write similar communications to Jewish communities, whose total population numbered only about two thousand at this time. Although it was Muslims who represented the ideal of inclusion, Jews and Catholics were often linked to them in early American debates about religious freedom, as George Washington and Thomas Jefferson and others fought for the rights of all non-Protestants.

136

Jefferson had an enlightened approach to religious liberty and tolerance that might cause us to think about our perceptions of Islamophobia. The fact is that Islam's presence in North America dates back to the founding of the nation, when Muslims arrived in North America as early as the 17th century as slaves from West Africa. It is estimated that about 20 percent of African slaves brought to the Americas were Muslim, including some with Arabic backgrounds (Denny, 2015). Muslims from the Middle East, mostly unskilled and uneducated laborers from the Syrian regions of the Arab world, did not immigrate here as free citizens until the late 19th century. The interest in Islam was exhibited by key Founding Fathers, most notably Thomas Jefferson, who demonstrated a marked interest in the faith and its followers.

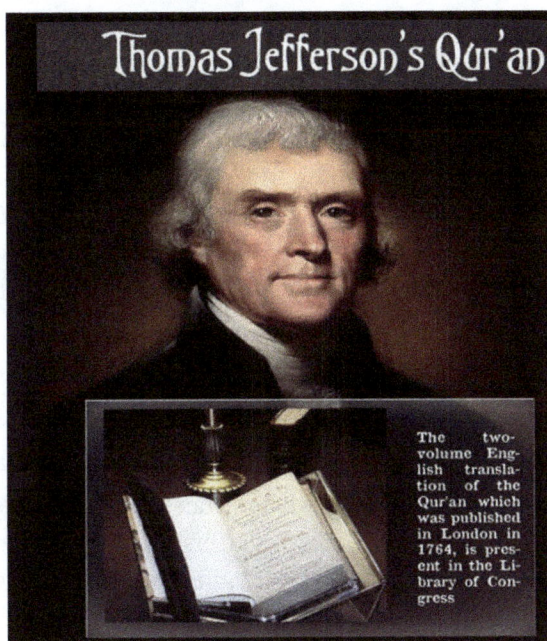

The two-volume English translation of the Qur'an which was published in London in 1764, is present in the Library of Congress

Figure 30: Thomas Jefferson and the Quran
Source: Library of Congress

Muslims were explicitly referenced by America's Founding Fathers, such as George Washington and Thomas Jefferson, who viewed them as potential citizens with rights and obligations no different from those of other Americans. They believed that Muslim immigrants and converts have helped to build America along with countless other groups of people. James Hutson wrote in his article The Founding Fathers and Islam, "Although there is no evidence that the Founders were aware of the religious convictions of their bondsmen, it is clear that the

Founding Fathers thought about the relationship of Islam to the new nation and were prepared to make a place for it in the republic" (Hutson, 2002).

In 2002, James Hutson, who was chief of the Library of Congress's Manuscript Division, noted the English philosopher John Locke had heavily influenced Jefferson's opinions on religious liberty. For example, in his Letter on Toleration in 1689 (see appendices), John Locke insisted that Muslims and all others who believed in God be tolerated in England. Later campaigning for religious freedom in Virginia, Jefferson followed Locke, his idol, in demanding recognition of the religious rights of the "Mahometans (Muslims)," the Jew and the "pagan." Supporting Jefferson was his old ally, Richard Henry Lee, who had made a motion in Congress on June 7, 1776, that the American colonies declare independence. "True freedom," Lee asserted, "embraces the Mahometans, and the Hindu as well as the Christian religion." This reflects that religious minorities and Muslims have been a part of that heated discussion from the very beginning of the nation's founding and their rights have been a feature of the nation's political discourse for centuries. Indeed, the key American Founding Fathers believed that religious liberty and political equality would not be exclusively Christian. In one of his private notes, Jefferson wrote, "neither Pagan nor Mahometan (Muslims) nor Jew ought to be excluded from the civil rights of the commonwealth because of his religion." This statement is a strong advocate for religious freedom, which he always supported and proclaimed, as "our civil rights have no dependence on our religious opinions."

In the Virginia Statute for Religious Freedom, which Jefferson authored, he emphasized Islam and wrote that the Mahometan should have his faith protected in the United States (Conversation, 2018). Jefferson, by this statement, meant that religious freedom should include every religion practiced in the United States. This clearly shows that Jefferson was thinking about Muslims at the time he was drafting the famous Virginia legislation. Indeed, we find evidence for this during the bill's debate when some legislators wanted to insert the name "Jesus Christ" in the bill. Jefferson strongly opposed this and argued he had intended the application of the statute to be "universal." By this, he meant that religious liberty and political equality would not be exclusively Christian.

Gestures to Muslims: Honoring Ramadan

Ideas about the nation's religiously plural character were tested also in Jefferson's presidential foreign policy with the Islamic powers of North Africa, when he welcomed the first Muslim envoy from Tunis to the White House in 1805. Because it was Ramadan, the Muslim holy month, the president moved the state dinner from 3:30 p.m. to be "precisely at sunset," in recognition of the Tunisian ambassador's Muslim beliefs. Ramadan is a holy month of fasting and prayer for Muslims. It is celebrated as the month during which Muhammad received the initial revelations of the Quran. Fasting is one of the five fundamental principles of Islam. Each day during Ramadan, Muslims do not eat or drink from dawn to sunset. Only after sunset do Muslims break their fast with a meal, referred to as an iftar. So how does a simple dinner invitation help bring Jefferson's perspective about Islam into the limelight? The courtesy of inviting a Muslim ambassador to a White House dinner during Ramadan and pushing back the time of a dinner by several hours shows Jefferson's respect for religious freedom and equality. While addressing the participants, Jefferson said the event was to celebrate the role of faith in the lives of the American people. He states, "They remind us of the basic truth that we are all children of God, and we all draw strength and a sense of purpose from our beliefs. The best way to honor the place of faith in the lives of our people was to protect their freedom to practice religion." Indeed, over the course of our American history, religion has thrived precisely because Americans have had the right to worship as they choose. The principle of religious freedom and equality has been upheld ever since. And it is a testament to the wisdom of our founders that America remains deeply religious, a country where people of different faiths can coexist peacefully and with mutual respect for one another while practicing their religious beliefs.

Since then, there has been a tradition of having an Iftar dinner at the White House. But the fact is that only three presidents in all of American history ever held an Iftar dinner. Bill Clinton held the first one in 1996 at a politically motivated dinner aimed at peeling Muslim voters away from the Republicans, since the growing Muslim-American community at the time leaned toward becoming a Republican constituency. President Clinton continued the tradition as did George Bush who hosted an Iftar dinner at the White House in 2001 in a diplomatic effort to prove the U.S. wasn't looking to go to war with all of Islam in the wake of the attacks on September 11, 20019 and the subsequent implementation of the war on terror. Bush continued the dinners every year of his two terms. Barack Obama hosted his first Iftar dinner in 2009, and subsequently every year of his presidency. The Iftar dinner in the White House become very popular event among Muslims and the event was widely discussed within Muslim communities nationwide and covered in the foreign press. This was the first time any administration acknowledged the Muslim community. Muslims felt good that someone at the highest level had invited them as a religious minority, included them, and appreciated them for the first time. It was a historic event for Muslims in the United States and abroad. However, anyone paying attention to Thomas Jefferson's Iftar dinner in 1805 would hear clearly that he had a vision for an America where Islam as a religion would be a part of American pluralistic fabric and that cannot be ignored. Thus, these events stem back to Thomas Jefferson, whose contribution to religious freedom and diversity should not be ignored.

For his 2010 Iftar dinner celebration, Obama said the following about Jefferson and Islam:

> *"Tonight, we are reminded that Ramadan is a celebration of a faith known for great diversity. And Ramadan is a reminder that Islam has always been part of America. The first Muslim ambassador to the United States, from Tunisia, was hosted by President Jefferson, who arranged a sunset dinner for his guest because it was Ramadan— making it the first known Iftar at the White House, more than 200 years ago." He continued, "This is America. And our commitment to religious freedom must be unshakeable. The principle that people of all faiths are welcome in this country and that they will not be treated differently by their government is essential to who we are. The writ of the Founders must endure."*

Hutson (2002), adhering to this point, wrote, "the Founders of this nation explicitly included Islam in their vision of the future of the republic. Freedom of religion, as they conceived it, encompassed it. Adherents of the faith were, with some exceptions, regarded as men and women who would make law-abiding, productive citizens." Far from fearing Islam, the Founders would have incorporated it into the fabric of American life. Thomas Jefferson and some of his allies explicitly mentioned Muslims in their speeches as they outlined the parameters of religious freedom and equal protection for American citizens.

Figure 31: *Iftar dinner at the White House in Washington on August 10, 2012*
Source: *Official White House Photo by Chuck Kennedy*

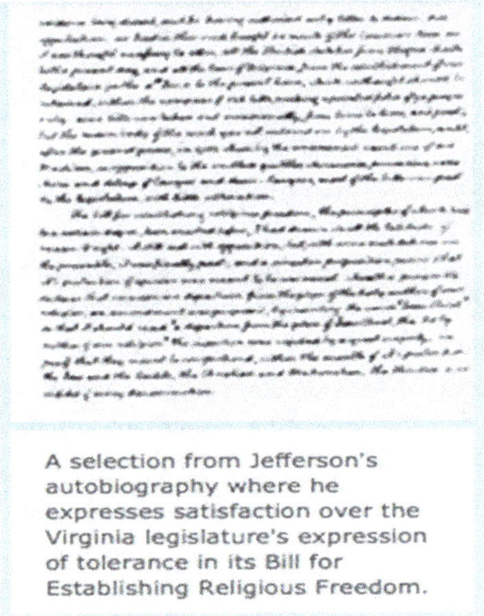

A selection from Jefferson's autobiography where he expresses satisfaction over the Virginia legislature's expression of tolerance in its Bill for Establishing Religious Freedom.

Figure 32: *Segment of Jefferson's autobiography*
Source: *Library of Congress*

Denise Spellberg argues (2013) in *Thomas Jefferson's Quran: Islam and the Founders* that to understand the state and the religion, we need to look to the Founders' views on Islam. Spellberg's point is that, contrary to those today who would reject Islam and Muslims as largely alien to the Americans values, politicians like Thomas Jefferson in the era of the nation's founding argued that the American Constitution should make room for Islam and for believing Muslims, a sentiment that existed about Muslims, who were not many in population in the colonies. This also tells us that Jefferson could imagine Muslims as future citizens of his new country (Spellberg, 2013).

While reviewing Spellberg's book, Professor Juliane Hammer at the University of North Carolina at Chapel Hill, argues that Thomas Jefferson's Quran examines the intersection during the nation's founding era of two contentious themes in the culture wars—the relationship of Islam to America, and the proper relationship between church and state. This legacy still continues in our democratic traditions today, where every religion is independent and practices its values regardless of any fear or concern. Hammer further argues that Keith Ellison, a Muslim Democrat from Minnesota, took his oath of office on January 3, 2007 with his hand on Jefferson's two-volume English translation of the Quran. When he announced his decision, controversy erupted from the conservatives and other like-minded people. This has revived the debate about whether America's values and legal system are shaped only by Judeo-Christian heritage or if there is room for Islam and other traditions.

Dennis Prager, who is Jewish and serves on the United States Holocaust Memorial Council, argued that Ellison should not be allowed to take his oath on the Quran. "America is interested in only one book, the Bible. If you are incapable of taking an oath on that book, don't serve in Congress." Prager, also a conservative talk radio host in Los Angeles, wrote a November 2006 column titled "America, not Keith Ellison, decides what book a Congressman takes his oath on" (Prager, 2006). In response to this criticism, Ellison said that Jefferson owned a Quran demonstrates from the very beginning of our country, we had people who were visionary, who were religiously tolerant, who believed knowledge and wisdom could be gleaned from any number of sources, including the Quran. He added, "A visionary like Thomas Jefferson was not afraid of a different belief system. This just shows that religious tolerance is the bedrock of our country, and religious differences are nothing to be afraid of" (Hammer, 2014). Spellberg argues that contrary to those today who would dismiss Islam and Muslims as essentially and irretrievably alien to the American experiment and its religious mix, key figures in the era of the nation's building, such as Thomas Jefferson whose interest in Islam promoted the vision that American church-state calculus both could and should make room for believing Muslims and their religion Islam. Jefferson further emphasized that "any attack upon the rights of Muslim citizens should be recognized for what it remains: an assault upon the universal ideal of civil rights promised all believers at the country's founding" (Spellberg, 2013). While Jefferson is best known for writing the Declaration of Independence in 1776, a few months later he also wrote the Virginia Statute for Religious Freedom for his native state Virginia, which served as a basis for the "no religious test" clause in the U.S. Constitution's Bill of Rights. In the Virginia statute he wrote, "The document demanded that all men shall be free to profess, and by argument to maintain, their opinion in matters of religion, and that the same shall in no way diminish, enlarge, or affect their civil capacities." The statute was drafted in 1777, became law in 1786, and inspired the Constitution's "no religious test" clause and the First Amendment.

The Constitution of the United States provides that "no religious Test shall ever be required as a Qualification to any Office or public Trust under the United States." During the ratification debates, a framer of the Constitution explained that this clause prohibits examination of "one's belief of certain doctrines ... for the purpose of determining whether his religious opinions are such, that he is admissible to a public office". The Declaration of Independence inspired many similar documents in other countries, the first being the 1789 Declaration of United Belgian States. It also served as the primary model for numerous declarations of independence in Europe and Latin America, as well as Africa (Liberia) and Oceania (New Zealand) during the first half of the 19th century.

It is believed the Quran's teaching about "compulsion" and "equality" inspired Jefferson. The Quran states there is no "compulsion" in (acceptance of) religion (Quran chapter 2 vs. 256). No compulsion means that no one has the right under God's system to force anyone else to follow or accept any religion. Each person has complete free will to follow the religion of their choice and the only one they are responsible to is God. Jefferson had asserted the principle of religious freedom in the Statute of Virginia in 1777. This statute summarized Jefferson's beliefs who was inspired by English philosopher John Locke. For Jefferson, the logic of religious freedom was inherent in the Enlightenment perspective, which asserts, "our civil rights have no dependence on our religious opinions." He saw freedom of religion as a "natural right" of man. He thought it was wrong to force an individual to belong to the establishment church, just as it was wrong for the state to suppress individual opinions.

Regarding equality, the U.S. Declaration of Independence, which Thomas Jefferson penned in 1776, also states, "all men are created Equal" and "men are born free." Similar phrases are mentioned in the Quran that states, "in the sight of Allah Almighty, all people are equal, but they are not necessarily identical". There are differences in abilities, potentials, ambitions, wealth, and so on. The foundations of this Islamic value of equality are deeply rooted in the structure of Islam. It stems from basic principles such as the following: "All men are created by One and the Same Eternal God, the Supreme Lord of all. And all people are born equal, in the sense that no one brings any possession with him; and they die equal in the sense that they take back nothing of their worldly belongings. God judges every person on the basis of his own merits and according to his own deeds." Jefferson, while drafting the Declaration of Independence, embedded this principle of equality in the Declaration.

Many social and political figures believe the Quran inspired Jefferson and he used the principles of equality and compulsion while working on the Declaration of Independence. Harvard University professor of Islamic history and culture, Ali Asani observed, "American Founding Fathers believe in religious tolerance as a key American ideal not only for various Protestant groups but also for its future and potential Muslim citizens of his new nation". Their tolerant attitude towards Catholics, Jews, and Muslims help us to understand the idea of religious freedom in the widest possible terms in the colonial times.

Jefferson's Quran was placed in the national spotlight in January 2007 when Keith Ellison, the United States' first Muslim congressman, swore his private oath of office on it instead of the customary Bible. Again, in January 2019, Rashida Tlaib, a new Muslim congresswoman, used Jefferson's Quran to repeat what Ellison had initiated. After the official swearing-in, Ellison, and later Tlaib, used Jefferson's Quran borrowed from the Library of Congress for a photo-op and said, the fact that Jefferson owned a Quran "demonstrates that from the very beginning of our country, we had people who were visionary, who were religiously tolerant and believed in equality, and that Islam has been part of American history." However, as I have mentioned earlier in the section, Jefferson himself endorsed the anti-Islamic views that were common in the colonies at that time. At the same time, he found that many things were common in Islam and Christianity. His exposure to Islamic piracy in the Mediterranean Sea (discussed below) during his presidency and the Muslim pursuit of bribes, tax, and ransom caused him to question their legitimacy as a religion. During the last few years of his life, his feelings about the Quran did not wane. As a matter of course, Jefferson viewed both the Quran and the Old Testament as sources of religious law, however, he did not use these sources in his private practice of law or his public practice of legislating. As Kevin Hayes, another eminent Jefferson scholar, wrote, "wanting to broaden his legal studies as much as possible, Jefferson found the Qur'an well worth his attention" (Hayes, 2008).

Barbary Wars 1801-1805

The following is a brief discussion of Jefferson's view on Islam and the Quran in the context of the Barbary states crisis that emerged at the turn of the 19th century. We will also look at how Jefferson tackled this crisis before and during his presidency.

When Thomas Jefferson was inaugurated in March 1801, the US was a new country, and desperately needed to utilize Atlantic trade routes in order to grow economically.

From the mid-1500s to the mid-1800s the North African countries of Morocco, Algeria, Tunisia, and Libya were called the Barbary States. They were autonomous provinces of the Ottoman Empire. These locations had their own leaders and operated like different countries. They developed a loose alliance and started a trade blockade in the Atlantic Ocean. Their naval forces operated like pirates on the open seas. Capturing merchant ships and enslaving or ransoming their crews provided the rulers of these nations with wealth and naval power. The only countries that were safe were those willing to pay a bounty. But even then, the pirates were ruthless, often increasing prices and taking prisoners, then demanding hefty ransoms. In March 1786, Thomas Jefferson and John Adams went to London to negotiate with Tripoli's envoy, ambassador Sidi Haji Abdrahaman. They asked him under what right he extorted money and took slaves in this way, and the ambassador explained that it was written in their Quran, that all nations, which had not acknowledged the Prophet, were sinners, whom it was the right and duty of the faithful to plunder and enslave; and that every mussulman (Muslim) who was slain in this warfare would go to paradise.

This conversation did not sound as if it came from someone who represents the true description of Islam. By interacting with the Muslim envoy and his aides, Jefferson began to understand the aggressive nature of Islam, hostility towards non-Muslims, forced conversion to Islam, the centrality of Jihad, and the heavenly reward for Jihadis slain in battle. And although Jefferson was an outspoken proponent of going to war against the Barbary states over their attacks on US shipping, he never framed his arguments for doing so in religious terms, sticking firmly to a position of political principle that ransom is incomprehensible to Americans. He also believed that religion should not be used to gain any advantage over an enemy during and after the war.

Although Jefferson, in his early political career, did criticize Islam as an "oppressive, dominating, and unscientific" religion, it was a charge he also leveled against Catholicism. He thought both religions fused religion and the state at a time he wished to separate them in his commonwealth. Despite his criticism of Islam, Jefferson supported the rights of its adherents, as he demonstrated in the Declaration of Independence and Virginia Statute of Religious Freedom. In both these documents, Jefferson's original legislative intent had been to include every one of every faith. Thus, his pluralistic vision was evident that he considered Muslims as a part of the new nation. Jefferson also showed an interest in Arabic language and bought several volumes of Arabic literature from his philosophy professor at William and Mary College, who had left Virginia for England during the Revolutionary War. His acquisition of Arabic literature further reflected his interest in Islam and its followers.

Figure 33: Barbary Wars 1801-1805
Source: William Bainbridge Hoff, 1878

Here we can also see Jefferson's different perspectives on Islam; on the one hand, he had a negative approach to Islam at this early stage. On the other hand, he could perceive the idea of Muslims as future citizens of the United States, and their civil rights, along with all other religious believers. This also tells us that Jefferson was a visionary who saw Muslims as a part of his new nation, practicing their civil rights and their religion along with other religions without fear or any threat. However, the tragic irony is that hatred of Islam and targeting Muslims around the world today is so widespread and unfortunately, this was not our forefathers' vision. But Jefferson's position on Muslim rights and potential for citizenship underscores the importance of Islam that remained consistent with his days as a law student in the 1760s until the end of his life in 1826.

CHAPTER 11

CONCLUSION AND DISCUSSION

The aim of the study is to establish a convincing overview on what is known about Islamophobia, its perpetrators, and reaction in the United States. On the basis of this study, it appears that the rise in Islamophobic sentiments since 2001 and particularly after 2016 presidential elections has become visible and widespread in American society.

The extreme feelings of prejudice, hatred, and fear towards Islam have led to the formation of hate groups towards Muslims following 9/11. Since then, numerous hate groups have emerged in the United States, with many different ideologies. The actions they take are usually violent and have a negative effect on American society. The Jewish question that was prominent in the 1930s and 1940s has become a Muslim question in the 21st century, calling Islam a major threat to American values. Islamophobic trends come in patterns of waves, particularly after the 2016 American presidential election. Since then, there has been a considerably higher level of Islamophobic attacks on Muslims in the United States and elsewhere. The use of words like "Islamic terrorism," Muslim ban, and Sharia laws mirrors that of President Trump's rhetoric about a so-called "immigrant invasion" posing threats to American jobs and safety.

Many hate groups have created hate organizations that believed in their own extremist ideologies. Many of these hate groups are supported by charity donations. Many big organizations have funded groups that openly support Islamophobia. In addition, the use of the Internet allows extremists to share ideas and strategies easily without people even needing to be involved with a specific group. These hate groups are often a form of terrorism, as they are using fear and intimidation to reach their end goal. The stereotypes formed around Muslims can be connected to the media's influence as well, since acts of violence committed by Muslims are more likely to be portrayed as terrorism in the media compared to those committed by other races. How can we disrupt the funding, organizing, and recruiting efforts of hate groups and the individuals involved in it? Why should terrorism have really harsh penalties but hate crimes that also injure or kill people do not? We need to make these crimes are more visible and hold perpetrators to account.

Some general trends

The increase of Islamophobic violence is influenced by several different factors, such as immigration, political climate, and discourse regarding anti-Muslim rhetoric, Islamophobic organizations, and the media coverage of Islamophobic hate crimes. The government and the political leadership need to take a stand on these types of offenses in order to prevent them from happening in the future. To do this, they should do a number of things. First, there should be more policing in areas where these hate groups have held meetings, committed crimes or hosted rallies. This can be achieved with undercover cops patrolling the area. The penalties for hate crimes need to be much more harsh than they currently are. These criminals need to learn the first time that their actions cannot be allowed to continue as they are putting other people at risk. There should be more awareness among young people when they are growing up. They need to understand it is perfectly fine to differ from other people. By instilling this in their heads from a young age, you may be able to reduce the number of racist/homophobes growing up. By taking a stand against these groups, there can be potential to reduce the amount of hate groups that currently exist in American society.

Since a great deal of Islamophobia is based on the notion that Muslims threaten the American way of life, values, and culture, one way to challenge these ideas is to highlight the many everyday roles Muslims occupy in American society. These Muslim men and women are strong, courageous, and determined to bring changes to their country. Instead of focusing on stereotypes and negative media narratives, we need to learn about Muslims and their religion Islam from literature and alternative media sources. Lastly, Muslim women are disproportionately affected by Islamophobic groups and their propaganda. They are not only seen as a threat to Western values, but they are also paradoxically portrayed as victims of an alleged Islamic sexism. Muslim women have done everything from becoming Pakistan's Prime Minister in Benazir Bhutto, to the first female Muslim to scale Mount Everest like Samina Baig, CEOs of startups, heads of banks, and everything in-between. Muslim women are leaving a mark in a way that Americans don't hear about in the media. Women are more involved in American society today than in the past. Traditionally, women were supposed to stay at home and take care of the family. However, Muslim women in the U.S. have more job opportunities, and they are willing to engage in the community. Here is one Muslim woman sharing her experience in the U.S.: "I had a lot of dreams in Iraq, but I never had a chance to make something of my dreams. When I came here to the United States, that was the first day I had a chance to do things.

This is the difference between my country and America," said Shati, 47, who graduated from university in Iraq but stayed home to raise her three sons. The distorted ideas about Muslims must be overturned with new narratives, led by Muslim women themselves, and presented via art, media, and popular culture to portray the diversity of their lives and their contribution to society. A Muslim woman, Sharmeen Obaid Chinoy from Pakistan, won two Oscars for producing art movies (one more than Leonardo DiCaprio). One was in 2012 for her documentary, *Saving Face* and another in 2016 for the biographical *A Girl in the River.*

Samina Ali, an Indian-born Muslim who lives in San Francisco, is the curator of "Muslima: Muslim Women's Art and Voices," which is a new global, online exhibition exploring what it means to be a Muslim woman today. In the process, she has challenged the existing perceptions and prejudices about gender, and history of dehumanization of women. Samina Ali believes Muslim women face two dilemmas; on the one hand, if they live in non-Muslim majority countries, they must face the stereotypes that dehumanize them. On the other hand, if they live in Muslim majority countries, they have to face laws or traditions or patriarchy that dehumanize them. Ali believes that through art and voices we can challenge these stereotypes. She seems to believe that the idea is to challenge the status quo and, hopefully, try to shatter pervasive prejudice and discrimination against women and to bring equality, self-esteem, and freedom of expression between genders.

Final comments

As we discussed in early chapters, 1 and 2, hate crimes are not an abnormality of current society, but rather a by-product of thrill-seeking individuals whose actions have been described as racist, xenophobic or right-wing extremist acts of violence in a society still coping with inequality, difference, fear, and hate (Perry (2001), and Mcdevitt and Bennett (2002). Attacks on worship places like Dar Al-Farooq Islamic Center and killing of innocent people like Balbir Singh Sodhi and many more is a testament of social reality that exist and reflect the widespread of anti-Islamic and anti-Muslim sentiments in the United States and elsewhere. Islamophobic hate crimes poses a great risk to the democratic foundations of the United States, as well as the coexistence of various cultures, which make America great. Both the political discourse and the civil society should acknowledge the seriousness of this issue and develop concrete strategies to counter Islamophobia.

Finally, as hate crimes and stereotypes targeting Muslims and other minorities proliferate across the United States, balanced and fair media reporting is needed more than ever. Technology enterprises, especially social media platforms, play an enormous role in the spread of hateful rhetoric and ideas, which can lead to the radicalization of people. Despite some good journalism practices, additional training and resources for media professionals and media organizations will help promote rights to equality and freedom of expression through democratic processes, which is essential to human dignity and contentment for a peaceful and happy life.

One example of this notion of human dignity and self-respect is expressed by Thomas Jefferson at the time of Declaration of Independence, on July 4, 1776:

> *"We hold these truths to be self-evident; that all men are created equal; that they are endowed by their creator with certain unalienable rights; that among these are life, liberty, and the pursuit of happiness."*

*RECENT UPDATE: INTERNATIONAL DAY TO COMBAT ISLAMOPHOBIA

On March 15, 2022, the United Nations General Assembly (UNGA) came together and adopted, by consensus, a resolution that created awareness on Islamophobia and the hatred towards minorities. The Assembly proclaimed March 15th as an International Day to Combat Islamophobia. The representative of Pakistan introduced the resolution and stressed that Islamophobia is a reality, noting that his country's Prime Minister, Imran Khan, has repeatedly raised international awareness about the growing phenomenon of Islamophobia and anti-Muslim hatred while practicing 'freedom of expression' and called for efforts to address the phenomenon. While quoting Imran Khan, he mentioned that hate speech, discrimination and violence are proliferating in several parts of world, causing great anguish in the Islamic world. Muslims often experience stigma, negative stereotyping and shame, feeling like suspect communities bearing collective responsibility for the actions of a radical few. The Pakistani representative continued that Islamophobia has emerged as a new form of racism, with an added gender aspect, as girls and women are targeted due to their dress and the notion that they are oppressed. Islamophobia is also finding purchase in the political sphere, including discriminatory travel bans and visa restrictions, and discourse among far-right groups for electoral gains. The situation remains poorly understood, he affirmed, with numerous world leaders, civil society and private sector underscoring the need to address it. "The objective of observing this day is about uniting, not dividing," the envoy said, concluding his address.

The General Assembly called for strengthened international efforts to foster a global dialogue on the promotion of a culture of tolerance and peace at all levels, based on respect for human rights and the diversity of religions and beliefs. That statement and the designation of an International Day is an important way to counter Islamophobia and its negative trends. Global action will help counter increasing acts of violence against Muslims around the world as well as discouraging the seriousness of phobias against all other religions and their followers. Here I would like to quote Canadian Prime Minister Justin Trudeau who has said that Islamophobia is "unacceptable" and stressed the need for putting an "end" to such hate against religious minorities as world leaders need to make effort to bridge the gap between different communities following hate attacks in the past. Also, President Putin's spoke publicly and vocally that disrespecting Islam and Prophet Muhammad is not freedom of expression, stressing the importance of spreading this message to leaders of the non-Muslim world to counter Islamophobia.

President Joe Biden in 2021 already supported the bill in the U.S. House of Representatives that requires the U.S. State Department to create a Special Envoy for monitoring and combating Islamophobia (the bill was passed by the House on December 14, 2021).

I believe that we should stand together against all forms of bigotry that must be condemned and tackled in all its aspects. Responding in a constructive way to hate crimes and standing in solidarity with the victims as discussed above is a step in the right direction to combat Islamophobia and racial discrimination faced by religious minorities around the world.

REFERENCES

ABC NEWS. (2016). Donald Trump Says He'll Consider Replacing Hijab-Wearing TSA Agents

With Veterans. Retrieved July 1, 2016 from https://abcnews.go.com/Politics/don ald-trump-request-rally-goer-replace-hijab-wearing/story?id=40269164

ACLU. 2017). Advocate for Immigrants' Rights in Your Community. Retrieved March 10, 2017 from https://www.aclu-in.org/en/news/advocate-immigr ants-rights-your-community/

Ahmed, S., & Matthes, J. (2016). 2000 to 2015: A meta-analysis. International Communication Gazette, 79(3), 219–244.

Ali, W. & Clifton, E. (2011). "Fear, Inc.: The Roots of the Islamophobia Network in America." Center for American Progress. Retrieved August 28, 2011, from https://www.americanprogress.org/issues/religion/reports/ 2011/08/ 26/10165/fear-inc/

Allen, C. (2001). Islamophobia in the media since September 11th. University of Westminster, London. UK.

All Party Parliamentary Group on Hate Crime. (2018). How do we build community cohesion when hate crime is on the rise? Retrieved from http://appghatecrime/wpuploads/2019/02/APPG%20o201Hate%20Crime %report

Allport, G.W. (1954). The nature of prejudice. Reading, MA: Addison-Wesley.

Anti-Defamation League. (2020). Act for America. https://www.adl.org/reso urces/profiles/act-for-aO00[0;/000/000/0/0merica/

Beirich, H. (February 20, 2019). The Year in Hate and Extremism. Southern Poverty Law Center. Retrieved March 18, 2019, from https://www.splc enter.org/fighting-hate/extremist-files/group/act-america/

Bell, K. (2017). Mark Zuckerberg slams neo-Nazis and 'polarization' after Charlottesville. Retrieved August 16, 2017 from https://mashable.com /article/mark-zuckerberg-charlottesville/

Bishop, T. (January 26, 2012). *Maryland man pleads guilty in terrorist bomb plot. The Baltimore Sun.* Retrieved from https://www.baltimoresun.com/latest/bs-md-co-martinez-plea-20120126-story.html

Bleich, E. (2011). What Is Islamophobia, and how much Is there? Theorizing and measuring an emerging comparative concept. *American Behavioral Scientist*, 55, 1581-1600.

Blumberg, A. (2017). A Brief History Of Donald Trump Stoking Islamophobia. Huffpost. Retrieved November 29, 2017 from https://www.huffpost.com/entry/donald-trump-islamophobia-history-n-5a1eeea2e4b01edb1a819c9e

Breen, C. D. (2012). Testing Criminological and Sociological Explanations for the Formation of Hate Groups. Ann Arbor. Temple University

Bureau of Justice Statistics. (2014). "U.S. residents experienced about 293,800 Hate crime victimizations in 2012. Unchanged from 2004." February 20, 2014. Washington, D.C.

Burke, D., & Hernandez, S. (2017, June 12). The four reasons people commit hate crimes.

Byers, B., Crider, B. W., & Biggers, G. K. (1999). Bias crime motivation: A study of hate crime offender neutralization techniques used against the Amish. *Journal of Contemporary Criminal Justice, 15 (1)*, 78–96.

Caldwell, P. (2016). Ben Carson says Islam is not a religion but a life organization system. Mother Jones. January 29, 2016.

CAIR. (2021). Reps Omar, Schakowsky Introduce Combating Global Islamophobia Bill [Press release]. https://www.omar.house.gov/

CAIR. (2016). Islamophobia and the Trump Team. January17, 2017. Council on American Islamic Relations. Washington, D.C.

CAIR. (2015). Blacklash Against American Muslims After Paris Attack. November 24, 2015. Council on American Islamic Relations. Washington, D.C.

CAIR. (2013). Financing Prejudice and Hate. Legislating Fear: Islamophobia and Its Impact in the United States January 2011-December 2012, Council on American-Islamic Relations, 2013, pp. 1–16

Caron, C. (2017). Victoria man charged with hate crime in burning of Mosque. New York Times. Retrieved from https://www.atf.gov/news/pr/victoria-man-gets.

Carter Center. (2017). Countering the Islamophobia Industry Toward More Effective Strategies Symposium, September 2017.

Ciftci, S. (2012). Islamophobia and threat perceptions: Explaining anti-Muslim sentiment in the West. Journal of Muslim Minority Affairs, 32(3), 293–309.

CNN. (2020) The four reasons people commit crimes. Retrieved November 14, 2020, from https://www.cnn.com/2017/06/02/us/who-commits-hate-crimes/index.html

CNN Wire Service. (November 20, 2016). "Explosion" in hate crimes since November 8th election prompts special New York police unit. www.fox6now.com/2016/11/20/explosion-in-hate-crimes-since-november-8th-election-p

Cohen, D. (February 23, 2017). Bill Maher's outrages statement about Islam and Muslims are beyond the pale. AlterNet.

Conversation. (2018). Why American's vision of American Islam matters today. The Conversation. February 19, 2018. Boston, MA.

C-SPAN. (2006). Jihad Watch. Retrieved from http://www.cspan.org/rebertsepencer/January 1, 2006.

C-SPAN. (2017). We need Better Hate Crime tracking. Anti-Defamation League Conference. Washington, D.C. May 8, 2017.

DeAngelis, T. (2001). Understanding and preventing hate crimes. Monitor on Psychology, American Psychological Association. November, 2001

Denny, F. (2015). An introduction to Islam. Publisher: Routledge; 4th edition. September 2015.

Department of Justice. (March 28, 2018). Wilmington man sentenced for threatening mosque and illegally possessing firearms and child pornography. Retrieved from https://www.justice.gov/usao-ma/pr/wilmington-man-sentenced-threatening-mosque-and-illegally-possessing-firearms-and-child

Economist. (2021). Muslims on top. The Economist. September 11, 2021.

Edwards, G., & Rushin, S. (2018). The elect of President Trump's election on hate crimes. Retrieved from https//paperds.ssm.com/sol3/papers.cfm?abst ractid=3102652

Egorova. Y. & Tudor, P. (2003). The dialogue between the European Union and the Islamic World in interreligious dialogues: Christians, Jews, and Muslims. Annals of the European Academy of Sciences and Arts, 24(10), 166–168.

Ekman, M. (2015): Online Islamophobia and the politics of fear: Manufacturing the green scare. Journal of Ethnic and racial Studies, 38 (11), 1986, 2002.

Emerson, S. (2002) "American Jihad: The Terrorist Living Among Us." In The Middle East Quarterly Vol. 9, No 3, 2002.

Epstein, R., & P. Nicholas. (2015). Donald Trump calls for ban on Muslim entry into U.S. Wall Street Journal. December 7, 2015. New York.

Evans, R. (2019). Ignore The Poway Synagogue Shooter's Manifesto: Pay Attention To 8chan's /Pol/ Board. Bellingcat. Retrieved April 28, 2019 from https://www.bellingcat.com/news/americas/2019/04/28/ignore-the-poway-synagogue- shooters-manifesto-pay-attention-to-8chans-pol-boa

Fadel, L. (2019). Mainstream Charities Are Unwittingly Funding Anti-Muslim Hate Groups. Retrieved May 7, 2019 from https://www.npr.org/2019/05/07/720832680/mainstream-charities-are-unwittingly-anti-muslim -hate-groups/

Farha, A. (September 18, 2003). Purveyors of Hatred: Muslims Who Fuel Islamophobia. New York Times. Retrieved from https://www.nytimes.co m/2003/09/18/opinion/IHT-_purveyors/

Fay, S (2021). An 'expert' Without Expertise | The Stanford Daily. https://www. stanforddaily.com/2017/11/09/an-expert-without-expertise/.

Federal Bureau of Investigation. (2016). Hate crimes against Muslims in US surge 67 percent. FBI Statistics [Online] Available: http://wwwfbi.gov/st ories/November 14, 2016.

Fisher, M. (February 18, 2015). Nine questions about the "Holy War" that Bill O'Reilly just declared. Vox Media. Retrieved from https://www.cnn.com/2018/10/29/tech/social-media-hate-speech

Fox, A. & Alvarez, M. (February 19, 2017). Trump Immigration Policies, Ban Protested at Times Square Rally. Newsday, 2017. Retrieved February 19, 2017 from https://www.newsday.com/news/new-york/trump-immigration/

Fuchs, C. (February 1, 2018). Reported Anti-Muslims Hate Incidents, Rhetoric Rose in Year after Election. News. Retrieved February 1, 2018, from https://www.nbcnews.com/news/asian- america/reported-anti/

Gabriel, B. (2010). "They Must Be Stopped." Publisher: St. Martin's Griffin. January 2010.

Gaffney, F. January, 2011. The Muslim Brotherhood is the Enemy, Big Peace. Retrieved from https://www.2011/01/30/the-Muslim-brotherhood-is-the-enemy/.

Gallup Inc. (2015). "Islamophobia: Understanding Anti-Muslim sentiment in the West."

Gallup.com, news.gallup.com/poll/157082/islamophobia-understanding-anti-mu slim-sentiment-west.aspx.

Gandel, S. (2019). Fidelity charitable fund bankrolls "hate groups," critics say. CBS News. Retrieved December 10, 2019, from https://www.cbsnews.com/news/fidelity-401k-provider-criticized-for-funding-hate-groups/

Gardner, K. (2018). Social Media: Where Voices of Hate Find a Place to Preach. Center for Public Integrity, 2018, from https://publicintegrity.org/politics/social-media-where-voices-of-hate-find-a-place- to-preach/.

Goldman, D. (October, 2018). Big Tech made the social media mess. CNN. Retrieved from https://www.cnn.com/2018/10/29/tech/social-media-hate-speech

Grossman, C. (2012). Number of U.S. mosques up 74% since 2000. USA Today. February 29, 2012.

Guardian, (2017). Leader of group widely identified as anti-Muslim meets with White House. March 21, 2017. London.

Guardian, (2016). "Michael Flynn will be a disaster as national security adviser." Richard Wollfe. November 19, 2016. London.

Guardian. (2015). Obama condemned Islamophobia in America. It's time Republicans did too. The Guardian. December 15, 2015.

Habib, S. (September 9, 2016). Islamophobia is on the rise in the US but so is Islam. MediaTenor. Retrieved from https://www.pri.org/stories/2016-09-09/muslims-america...

Hammer, J. (April 9, 2014). Thomas Jefferson's Quran. In Religion and Politics, Washington University. St. Louis. Retrieved April 9, 2014 from https://www.religionandpolitics.org/tag/islams:/

Harvard Gazette, (2021). Muslim Americans who endured post-9/11 bias see solutions in education, political involvement. Liz Mineo. September 9, 2021. Cambridge, MA.

Hayes, J. Kevin (2008). The Road to Monticello: The Life and Mind of Thomas Jefferson. New York: Oxford University Press, 2008.

Horowitz, D. (2004). Unholy Alliance: Radical Islam and the American Left. Washington, DC: Regnery Publishing, Inc.

Howard, J. (2019). Free speech and hate speech. Annual Review of Political Science, 22, 93–109. *ISPU. American Muslim Poll 2017: Key findings. Institute for Social Policy and Understanding.* Retrieved June 14, 2018, *from https* www.ispu.org/american-muslim-poll-2017-key-findings.

Hutson, J. H. (2002) Religion and the Founding of the American Republic. 1998. Library of Congress Information Bulletin, May 2002, Vol. 61, No. 5

Jenkins, J. (2017). As anti-Islam incidents rise, Muslim groups take step to prevent arson. Thinkprogress. May 11, 2017.

Kaleem, J. (2016). Islam in America: Dramatic increase in just over a decade. Huffpost. February, 29, 2012.

Kanji, A. (2018). Framing Muslims in the "War on Terror": Representations of Ideological Violence by Muslim versus Non-Muslims Perpetrators in Canadian National News Media. In Religion, Vol. 9, No. 9. p 274.

Katayoun, K. (November, 2017). Assaults against Muslims in U.S. surpass 2001 level. Pew Research Center. Retrieved from https://www.pewresearch. org/staff/katayoun-kishi

Kazeem, H. (2016). Funding Islamophobia: $206m went to promoting 'hatred' of American Muslims. Retrieved June 20, 2016 from https://www.thegu ardian.com/us-news/2016/jun/20/islamophobia-funding-cair-berkeley-report

Kearns, E., & Allison, B. (April 18, 2019). Analysis, Yes, the media do underreport some terrorist attacks. Just not the ones most people think of. The Washington Post. Retrieved from https://papers.ssrn.com/sol3/papers. cfm?abstractid=2928138

Kearns, E., M., Betus, A., & Lemieux, A. (February, 2019). Why do some terrorist attacks receive more media attention than others? Justice Quarterly, 36(16), 1-24.

Klass, B. (2019). Opinion/ A short history of President Trumps Anti-Muslim bigotry. The Washington Post, WP Company May 15, 2019.

Klein, E. (2019). The media amplifies Trump's racism. Should it stop? Vox. Retrieved from https://www.vox.com/policy-andpolitics/2019/8/2/20702 029/donald-trump-racism-squad-tweets-media-2020

Kotch, A. (2019). America's Biggest Charities Are Funneling Millions to Hate Groups From Anonymous Donors. Retrieved February 19, 2019 from https://readsludge.com/2019/02/19/americas-biggest-charities-are-funneli ng-millions-to-hate-groups-from-anonymous-donors/

Laub, Z. (June 7, 2019). Hate speech on social media. Global comparisons. Council on Foreign Relations. Retrieved from https://www.cfr.org/back grounder/hate-speech-social..

Levin, B. (2018). Explaining the rise in hate crimes against Muslims in the U.S. The Conversation. Retrieved September 19, 2018, from https://www.sthec onversation.com/explaining-the-rise-hate-crimes-against-muslims-in- the-us- 80304/

Lichtblau, E. (September 17, 2016). Hate crimes against Muslims most since post 9/11 era. New York Times. Retrieved from https www.cambridge. org/core/journals/politics-and..tps:

Lisignoli, Maria. "Anti-Muslim Hate Crimes Increase after 9/11, Madison Muslim Community Unites against Hate." Https://Www.nbc15.Com, NBC News, 10 Sept. 2021, https://www.nbc15.com/2021/09/10/anti-mu slim-hate-crimes-increase-after-911-madison-muslim-community-unites-against-hate/.

Main. D. (July 26, 2016). Wilmington man charged with threatening local mosque on Facebook. Fox 25. Retrieved from https://www.bostonglobe. com/metro/2016/07/26/feds-charge.

Mark, P. (February 15, 2017). The Year in Hate and Extremism. Southern Poverty Law Center. Retrieved February 11, 2018 from https://www.www.splcen ter.org/.../2017-year-hate-and-extremism/

McAndrew, T (2021). The History of the KKK in American Politics - JSTOR Daily. https://daily.jstor.org/history-kkk-american-politics/.

McDevitt, J., J. Levin, and S. Bennett (2002). Hate crime offenders: An expanded typology. Journal of Social Issues, 58 (2), 303–317.

Mehdi, H. (April 9, 2009). Know your enemy. New Statesman. Retrieved from https://www.newstatesman.com/2009/07/mehdi-hasan-muslim.

Miller, C. (October 12, 2015). Social media is driving the rise of hate crime, but it can also stop it. The Telegraph. Retrieved from https://www.telegraph. co.uk/news/uknews/crime/11925950/...

Moscowwitz, P. (2016). We can fight back against Trump's Islamophobia. Nation. November 8, 2016. New York.

Nazarian, A. (November 16, 2015). ISIS is a direct threat to the United States. Breitbart News Daily. Retrieved from https://www.breitbart.com/politics /2015/11/16/amb-john..

Nealey, P. (2014). Why they join? Retrieved February 25, 2014 from https://www.splcenter.org/fighting-hate/intelligence-report/2014/why-they-join/

Newsday (2017). Trump immigration policies, ban protested at Times Square rally. https://www.newsday.com/news/new-york/trump-immigration-poli cies-ban-protested-at- times-square-rally-1.13147060.

New York City Council. (2016). Caucus and over 500 elected officials speak out against anti-Muslim bigotry. New York City Council Member Ben Kallos office. Press release. Thursday September 29, 2016.

No Author, (2017). David Yerushalmi. Southern Poverty Law Center. Retrieved June 2017 from https://www.splcenter.org/fighting-hate/extremist-files /individual/david-yerushalmi

No Author, (2017). "Funding Hate," Anti-Defamation League. Retrieved December 5, 2017 from https://www.adl.org/sites/default/files/documen ts/adl-report-funding-hate-how-white-supremacists-raise-their-money/

O'Brian. (2017). Twitter's plan to police hate speech and symbols. Retrieved October 17, 2017 from https://money.cnn.com/2017/10/17/technology/bu siness/twitter-content-modera

Oded, Y. (2018). Islamophobia permeated mainstream U.S. media. Retrieved from www.fairplanet.org/editors-pick/islamophobia-permeates-mainstrea m-u-s-media/

Panagopoulos, C. (2006). The polls trends: Arab and Muslim Americans and Islam in the aftermath of 9/11. Public Opinion Quarterly, 70 (4), 608–624.

Pandit, Idrisa. "Special Issue 'Anti Muslim Racism and the Media.'" Religions | Special Issue: Anti-Muslim Racism and the Media. Retrieved Aug. 2018, from https://www.mdpi.com/journal/religions/special_issues/-media/

Parillo, N. (2015). Diversity in America. Boulder, CO: Paradigm Publishers.

Peek, L. (2012). Behind the Backlash: Muslims Americans after 9/11. Temple University Press.

Perry, B. (2001). In the name of hate: Understanding hate crimes. New York: Routledge.

Pew Research Center. (2021). "Women are becoming more involved in U.S. mosques". *Mohamed Basheer.* August 4, 2021. Washington, D.C.

Pew Research Center. (2021). Negative biases toward U.S. Muslims, Islam have become more partisan. Stef W. Kight. September 8, 2021. Washington, D.C.

Pew Research Center. (2018). New Estimates show U.S. Muslim population continues to grow. Besheer Mohammad. January 3, 2018. Washington, D.C.

Pew Research Center. (2017). In many ways, Muslim men and women see life in America differently. Claire Gecewicz. August 7, 2017. Washington, D.C.

Pew Research Center. (2014). American Muslim perspective. Annual Report. September 9, 2011. Washington, D. C.

Pew Research Center. (2011). No signs of growth in alienation or support for extremism. Survey Report. August 30, 2011. Washington, D.C.

Powell, B. (2013). Fox News racial crime coverage is hurting people. Media Matters for America. Retrieved from https://www.mediamatters.org/fox-friends/fox-news-racial..

Prager, D. (November 28, 2006). "America, not Keith Ellison, decides what book a congressman takes his oath on". *Retrieved December 4, 2006 from https:/www.en.wikipedia.org/wik/quran*

Rao, K., Shenkman, C., Ahmed, K., Nisar, H., Mogahed, D., Buageila, S...Grimes, K. (2018). Equal treatment? Measuring the legal and media responses to ideologically motivated violence in the United States. Retrieved from https://www.imv-report.org

Said, E. (1997). *Covering Islam: How the media and the experts determine how we see the rest of the world.* New York, NY: Random House.

Schwab Caritable, 2018. Schwab Charitable Reports Record Grants in 2017 Amid Unique Charitable Giving Landscape. Retrieved May 7, 2019 from https://www.npr.org/2019/05/07/720832680/mainstream-charities-are-unwittingly-funding-anti-muslim-hate-groups/

Scott, E. (November 20, 2015). Ben Carson compares some refugees to 'rabid' dogs. CNN. Retrieved from https://www.cnn.com/2015/11/19/politics/ben-carson-rabid.

Shaheen, J. (2014). Reel bad Arabs: How Hollywood vilifies a People. Interlink Publishing Group. 2014.

Sinclair Broadcast Group. (April 12, 2016). Mosques experiencing growth in U.S. Retrieved from https://www.wjla.com/.../mosques-experiencing-grow th-in-us

Smith, M. B. (February 13, 2013). Islam is Demonic, Not a Religion, But an Economic System. Huff Post. Retrieved February 14, 2013, from https:/www.huffpost.com/entry/pat- robertson- claims/

Southern Poverty Law Center. (2021). 20 years after 9/11, Islamophobia continues to haunt Muslims. Kiara Alfonseca. Retrieved September 11, 2021 from https://www.splcenter.org/fighting-hate/extremist-files/ideolo gy/anti-muslim.

Southern Poverty Law Center. (2016). Incidents of hateful harassments since election day. Hatewatch Staff. Retrieved from https://www.nbcnews.com/n ews/us-news/southern-poverty.

Spellberg A. D. (2013). Thomas Jefferson's Quran: Islam and the Founders. Vintage Press, New York. Knopf Doubleday Publishing Group.

Stainburn, S. (2012). 74% more mosques in America since 2000: survey. The World, *Retrieved from https://www.pri.org/stories/2012-02-29/74-more-mosques-america-2000-survey*

Tashman, B. (August, 2016). Islam is a Cancer and a political ideology that hides behind a religion. Right Wing Watch.

Toppo, G. (2017). 'I am a Muslim Too' rally protests travel ban. USA Today. Retrieved February 19, 2017, from https://www.usatoday.com/story/news /2017/02/19/nyc/

United Nations News. (2021). Anti-Muslim hatred has reached epidemic proportions. Human Rights. Retrieved from https://news.un.org/en/story/ 2021/03/1086452

U.S. Bureau of the Census. (2016). America Muslim population. Government Printing Press, Washington, D. C.

U.S. Department of Justice. (2021). Two California men indicted in hate crimes case alleging they attacked family-owned restaurant and threatened to kill the owner. Retrieved April 27, 2021, from https://www.justice.gov/opa/pr/two-california-men-indicted-hate-crimes-case-alleging-they-attacked-family-owned-restaurant/

U.S. Department of Justice. (2020). Federal jury convicts Illinois man for bombing the Dar Al Farooq Islamic Center. Retrieved December 9, 2020 from https://www.justice.gov/usao-mn/pr/federal-jury-convicts-illinois-man-bombing-dar-al-farooq-islamic-center

U.S. Islamophobia Network Organizations. (2018). Retrieved October 30, 2020, from http://www.islamophobia.org/islamophobia-network/organizations.htm/

USA Today. (2012). Number of U.S. mosques up 74% since 2000. Cathy Grossman. February 29, 2012.

Walker, K. (2017). Four steps we're taking today to fight terrorism online. Retrieved June 18, 2017 from https://blog.google/around-the-globe/google- euro pe/four-steps-were-taking-today-fight-o/

Weber, B. (July 18, 2018). When Trump tweets about Muslims, hate crimes increase. Big Think. Retrieved July 18, 2018 from https://www.bigthin k.com/brandon-weber/dog-whistles-indeed/

William, P. (2013). Mike Huckabee goes all-in on Islamophobia, calls Muslims animals. MIC. Pierce William. August 8, 2013.

Woolfe, S. (May 7, 2018). The role of the media in the spread of Islamophobia. *Retrieved from https://www.samwoolfe.com/2018/05/the-role-of-the-med ia-in-the-spread-of-islamophobia.html*

Yadidi, N. (June 29, 2017). Majority of hate crimes goes unreported. CNN. Retrieved from https://www.edition.cnn.com/.../doj-hate-crime-report/in dex.html

Yan, H. (2015). Garland shooting: What is the American Freedom Defense Initiative? CNN. Retrieved November 14, 2020, from https://www.cnn.com/2015/05/04/us/what-is-american-freedom-defense-initiative/ind ex.html/

Yin, R. (1989). Case study Research, Design and Methods. Revised edition. Applied Social Research Methods Series. 5, London, UK: Sage Publications.

Zúquete, J. P. (2008). The European extreme-right and Islam: New directions?

APPENDICES

1. List of Organizations/groups/bodies

The Daily Show
Islamic State of Iraq and Syria (ISIS)
U.S. Bureau of Census (USBC)
Pew Research Center (PEW)
USA Today
The Economist
National Football League (NFL)
English Premier League
Flex-N-Gate
Five Pillars of Islam
C-SPAN
Medinah Academy of Madison
Think Progress
Bureau of Justice Statistics (BJS)
Southern Poverty Law Center
(SPLC)
The Guardian
The Institute for Social Policy (ISPU
Sinclair Broadcast Group (SBG)
Fox News
CBS News
NBC News
CNN
Twitter
Facebook
LinkedIn
Instagram
The United States Department of
Justice (USDJ)
Federal Bureau of Investigation
(FBI)
Center for American–Islamic
Relations (CAIR)
The New Statesman

All Party Parliamentary Group on
Hate Crimes (APPGHC
Mother Jones
Media Tenor
United Nations Human Rights
Council
American House of Representatives
The Carter Center
Emory University
Local Progress (LP)
Young Elected Officials Action
Network (YEO Action)
New York City Council
U.S. Council of Muslim
Organizations (USCMO)
Islamic Society of North America
(ISNA)
Muslim Public Affairs Council
(MPAC)
Islamic Circle of North America
(ICNA)
Suffolk police academy
White Rabbit Militia Group
The Republican Party
Gallup Organization
Transport Security Administrating
ABC Television News
The Proud Boys
Bureau of Justice Statistics (BJS)
Al Qaida
The White House
American Civil Liberties Union
(ACLU)

All Party Parliamentary Group on Hate Crimes (APPGHC)
The American Center for Law and Justice
The American Freedom Defense Initiative
Dar Al-Farooq Islamic Center
The Middle East Forum
The Family Research Council
Donors Capital Fund and Donors Trusted
Alan and Hope Winters Family Foundation
Scaife Foundation
Russell Berrie Foundation
Fairbook Foundation Newton, D. & Rochelle Foundation and Charitable Trust
William Rosenwald Family Fund, Middle Road Foundation, and Abstraction Fund
Lynde and Harry Bradley Foundation
Fidelity Charitable
Schwab Charitable
David Horowitz Freedom Center
Frank Gaffney's Center for Security Policy
The Internal Revenue Service (IRS)
The Counterterrorism & Security Education and Research Foundation
American Islamic Forum for Democracy
Middle East Forum
Investigative Project on Terrorism

Jihad Watch
Islamist Watch project
Center for Security Policy Society of Americans for National Existence
Family Research Council
Investigative Project on Terrorism
Clarion Project
ACT for America Education
Anti-Defamation League
Aryan Brotherhood
Identity Europa
Ku Klux Klan
The Coalition Against Islam
Big Peace Blog
Feeding America
Society of Americans for National Existence (SANE)
Youtube
The Red Cross
Planned Parenthood
Salvation Army
Doctors Without Borders
Campus Watch
Discover the Networks
Foundation for Ethnic Understanding (FFEU)
The Jamaica Muslim Center.
Movement to End Racism and Islamophobia (MERI)
The New York Immigration Coalition
Make the Road New York
Chanukah Action Against Islamophobia and Racism
Library of Congress

2. Resolutions

Resolutions passed in City Councils:
Tucson, AZ; City of Cudahy, CA; Culver City, CA; Oakland, CA; Richmond, CA; San Francisco, CA; West Hollywood, CA; Washington, DC; Miami, FL; Chicago, IL; Indianapolis, IN; New Orleans, LA; Cambridge, MA; Springfield, MA; Baltimore, MD; Montgomery County, MD; Portland, ME; Minneapolis, MN; Kansas City, MO; St. Louis City, MO; Durham, NC; Greensboro, NC; The County of Union, NJ; New York, NY; Village of Ossining, NY; Rochester, NY; Bowling Green, OH; Columbus, OH; Borough of Dormont, PA; Philadelphia, PA; City of Bolivar, TN; Austin, TX; Tacoma, WA, and Tukwila, WA

Resolutions passed in School Districts:
Creighton Elementary School District, AZ; Osborne School District, AZ; Tolleson Unified School District, AZ; Anaheim Unified High School District, CA; Franklin-McKinney School Board, CA; Garvey School District, CA; Lynnwood Unified School District, CA; Santa Clara County Board of Education, CA; Vallejo School Board, CA; Lovington Municipal School District, NM; Rochester City School District, NY; Metro Nashville Public School Board, TN

3. Painting "Mural" and the related links

Background information for the figures in the middle can be found in these links:

- ✓ http://www.cnn.com/2015/02/11/us/chapel-hill-shooting/

- ✓ http://www.independent.co.uk/news/world/europe/aylan-kurdi-s-story-how-a-small-syrian-child-came-to-be-washed-up-on-a-beach-in-turkey-10484588.html

- ✓ https://www.theguardian.com/world/2016/aug/18/boy-in-the-ambulance-image-emerges-syrian-child-aleppo-rubble

4. John Locke Letter Concerning Toleration 1689

Honoured Sir,

Since you are pleased to inquire what are my thoughts about the mutual toleration of Christians in their different professions of religion, I must needs answer you freely that I esteem that toleration to be the chief characteristic mark of the true Church. For whatsoever some people boast of the antiquity of places and names, or of the pomp of their outward worship; others, of the reformation of their discipline; all, of the orthodoxy of their faith - for everyone is orthodox to himself - these things, and all others of this nature, are much rather marks of men striving for power and empire over one another than of the Church of Christ. Let anyone have never so true a claim to all these things, yet if he be destitute of charity, meekness, and good-will in general towards all mankind, even to those that are not Christians, he is certainly yet short of being a true Christian himself. "The kings of the Gentiles exercise leadership over them," said our Saviour to his disciples, "but ye shall not be so."[1] The business of true religion is quite another thing. It is not instituted in order to the erecting of an external pomp, nor to the obtaining of ecclesiastical dominion, nor to the exercising of compulsive force, but to the regulating of men's lives, according to the rules of virtue and piety. Whosoever will list himself under the banner of Christ, must, in the first place and above all things, make war upon his own lusts and vices. It is in vain for any man to unsurp the name of Christian, without holiness of life, purity of manners, benignity and meekness of spirit. "Let everyone that nameth the name of Christ, depart from iniquity."[2] "Thou, when thou art converted, strengthen thy brethren," said our Lord to Peter.[3] It would, indeed, be very hard for one that appears careless about his own salvation to persuade me that he were extremely concerned for mine. For it is impossible that those should sincerely and heartily apply themselves to make other people Christians, who have not really embraced the Christian religion in their own hearts. If the Gospel and the apostles may be credited, no man can be a Christian without charity and without that faith which works, not by force, but by love. Now, I appeal to the consciences of those that persecute, torment, destroy, and kill other men upon pretence of religion, whether they do it out of friendship and kindness towards them or no? And I shall then indeed, and not until then, believe they do so, when I shall see those fiery zealots correcting, in the same manner, their friends and familiar acquaintance for the manifest sins they commit against the precepts of the Gospel; when I shall see

---

[1] Luke 22. 25, http://www.let.rug.nl/usa/documents/1651-1700/john-locke-letter-concerning-toleration-1689.php

[2] II Tim. 2. 19, http://www.let.rug.nl/usa/documents/1651-1700/john-locke-letter-concerning-toleration-1689.php

[3] Luke 22, http://www.let.rug.nl/usa/documents/1651-1700/john-locke-letter-concerning-toleration-1689.php. 32.

them persecute with fire and sword the members of their own communion that are tainted with enormous vices and without amendment are in danger of eternal perdition; and when I shall see them thus express their love and desire of the salvation of their souls by the infliction of torments and exercise of all manner of cruelties. For if it be out of a principle of charity, as they pretend, and love to men's souls that they deprive them of their estates, maim them with corporal punishments, starve and torment them in noisome prisons, and in the end even take away their lives - I say, if all this be done merely to make men Christians and procure their salvation, why then do they suffer whoredom, fraud, malice, and such-like enormities, which (according to the apostle)*(4)[4] manifestly relish of heathenish corruption, to predominate so much and abound amongst their flocks and people? These, and such-like things, are certainly more contrary to the glory of God, to the purity of the Church, and to the salvation of souls, than any conscientious dissent from ecclesiastical decisions, or separation from public worship, whilst accompanied with innocence of life. Why, then, does this burning zeal for God, for the Church, and for the salvation of souls - burning I say, literally, with fire and faggot - pass by those moral vices and wickednesses, without any chastisement, which are acknowledged by all men to be diametrically opposite to the profession of Christianity, and bend all its nerves either to the introducing of ceremonies, or to the establishment of opinions, which for the most part are about nice and intricate matters, that exceed the capacity of ordinary understandings? Which of the parties contending about these things is in the right, which of them is guilty of schism or heresy, whether those that domineer or those that suffer, will then at last be manifest when the causes of their separation comes to be judged of He, certainly, that follows Christ, embraces His doctrine, and bears His yoke, though he forsake both father and mother, separate from the public assemblies and ceremonies of his country, or whomsoever or whatsoever else he relinquishes, will not then be judged a heretic.

---

[4] Rom. I., http://www.let.rug.nl/usa/documents/1651-1700/john-locke-letter-concerning-toleration-1689.php

INDEX

Quranic learning, 41

ABOUT THE AUTHOR

Early Growth and Education

Navid Ghani was born in Lahore, Pakistan, to a highly educated middle-class family.

His parents taught him tolerance and respect for other people's religion and beliefs. His parents are not alive now, but they live in his memories, and he is thankful to them for providing him with the best education and values one could receive. It was because of their encouragement and support that he migrated twice to pursue higher studies, first to Norway and then to the United States. As of this writing, his siblings, three sisters, and a brother (late) are scattered over three different continents, where they live happily with their families.

Ghani's lifelong pursuit of self-improvement began at a young age. He received his first master's degree with honors in historiography from the Punjab University, Pakistan. Then he moved to Northern Europe, specifically to Norway, to study Nordic socioeconomic and cultural history. He got his second master's degree from the University of Oslo in 1980 (the first ever Asian in Norway to do so). As a topic for his master's thesis, he focused on "State Ownership as an Element of Mixed Economy." He wanted to research the role played by the state in creating the element of a mixed economy and the concept of welfare state in postwar Norway. The term "mixed economy" describes, in general terms, an economic system that is neither state capitalism nor a traditional free market economy, but rather a system where state control and a market economy exist together, side-by-side, in a constant state of mutual accommodation and adjustment that stems from understanding and practical cooperation.

To further pursue higher education, he moved to the United States from Norway in 1996, where he was awarded a third master's degree in 1999 from Stony Brook University, New York. He attained a PhD in sociology in 2003 from the same university in 2003 in the areas of immigration and race relations.

Moving to Norway

Norway is situated in the Western section of the Scandinavian Peninsula and shares borders with Sweden, Finland, and Russia. Norway (or *Norge*) means "the northern way"). The country is situated at almost the same northern latitude as Alaska. However, the climate is more temperate than its northern latitude might indicate because of warming from the Gulf Stream. Most of Norway's population descends from Caucasian German tribes that came to the area from the south about two thousand years ago. Known as Nordic, the Norwegian people are tall, and most have blonde hair, blue eyes, and long angular faces. Norway has two official and similar languages, *bokmål* and *nynorsk*. The latter has its origin in rural dialects, whereas *bokmål* reflects the language of the cities, influenced by Denmark during its four hundred year reign over Norway. All government institutions are mandated to use both languages.

In spite of demographic changes in recent years, Norwegian society is relatively homogenous. It has one school system, one state church, one ethnic heritage, one king, and, until recently, one television and broadcasting company. It also has a rather low immigration rate. Norwegian society's homogeneity was a bit of a surprise to Ghani at first when he was a newcomer in the early 1970s. He noticed that, whenever he was in public spaces, he would be confronted with rows of similar blonde heads and blue-eyed people around him. In the university cafeteria, students ate identical lunches composed of white bread spread with butter and white and brown cheese.

Norwegians describe themselves as "average," perhaps as a way of de-emphasizing any special status. If you ask a Norwegian about their socioeconomic status, they will proudly say, "I am an average person." In contrast, immigrants originating from societies with a hierarchical social order view honors and status as a symbol of prestige and respect. This differing perspective becomes problematic for many immigrants as they try to adjust to Norwegian society.

Unlike many other European countries, Norway does not have a history of colonization, nor has it been a land of immigration like the United States and Canada. Norway's history as an immigrant country is relatively recent. From 1945 onward, immigration to Norway was limited to 3,000–4,000 annually. Most of the postwar immigrants came from the Nordic countries, such as Sweden, Finland, and Denmark. However, the economic growth of the late 1960s brought immigrants from Western Europe and the United States. Many of them were experts in the gas and oil industry, and Norway needed such people because of the discovery of oil

180

in the North Sea. Additionally, a high level of growth demanded, in turn, a larger workforce. Norway therefore encouraged the migration of labor from Turkey, Pakistan, and other non-European countries. The first Pakistani group of ten men arrived in Oslo in 1967. By 1971, the number had grown to 110 men, including Ghani himself, and it continued to rise to 990 by the following year. In 2019, the total Pakistani population in Norway was about 38,000.

To backtrack a bit, when Dr. Ghani researched the Norwegian model of mixed economy for his master's thesis, in Oslo, he happened to meet the Norwegian "father of the nation" Einar Gerhardsen, who had been the prime minister of post-war Norway and the architect behind the concept of the mixed economy for more than 20 years. When Dr. Ghani first asked him for an interview, he replied, "Navid, I cannot speak English, but if you can speak Norwegian, then it is great. If not, then we have to arrange for an interpreter."

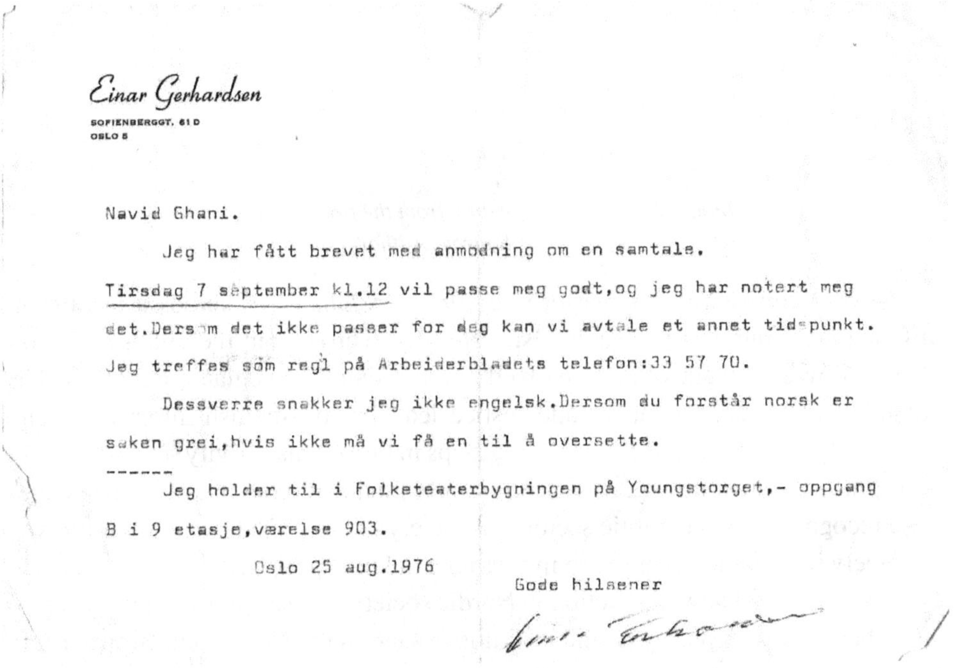

Einar Gerhardsen
SOFIENBERGGT. 61 D
OSLO 5

Navid Ghani.

Jeg har fått brevet med anmodning om en samtale.

Tirsdag 7 september kl.12 vil passe meg godt,og jeg har notert meg

det.Dersom det ikke passer for deg kan vi avtale et annet tidspunkt.

Jeg treffes som regl på Arbeiderbladets telefon:33 57 70.

Dessverre snakker jeg ikke engelsk.Dersom du forstår norsk er

saken grei,hvis ikke må vi få en til å oversette.

Jeg holder til i Folketeaterbygningen på Youngstorget,- oppgang

B i 9 etasje,værelse 903.

Oslo 25 aug.1976

Gode hilsener

Image 1: Invitation from the prime minister (in Norwegian)
Source: *Author*

Dr. Ghani liked his straightforwardness and honestly. However, they talked without an interpreter, because, by then, Ghani was quite fluent in the Norwegian language. Long after their meeting, Gerhardsen regularly sent Dr. Ghani Christmas greeting cards each year. In December 1985, he received his last greeting card. He died in 1986. To this day, Dr. Ghani kept them all as good memories.

Julen 1985 .

```
Kjære Navid Ghani.
Takk for kort og hilsen.
-------
Får jeg ønske deg alt godt for
julen og det nye året.
-------
Ring meg på nyåret for å få avtalt
en samtale.Jeg treffes enten på
Arbeiderbladets telefon:42 93 80 -
eller privat:19 91 11.

        Gode hilsener
```

Image 2: Christmas greeting from the prime minister (1985)
Source: Author

After completing his master's in 1980, Dr. Ghani worked as a lecturer in different academic institutions in Oslo, Norway. Throughout the 1980s and early 1990s, he was very active and involved in the Asian–Norwegian community. His commitment to racial equality and justice led him to establish information and community centers for different ethnic groups in Oslo. This activity set a precedent, as, for the first time, immigrants' needs for communication in their own languages were recognized by the public sector and society at large. These initiatives proved extremely invaluable because the immigrants did not speak the local language and did not understand how to function in Nordic society. These contributions occurred while he was employed by public institutions such as the Norwegian Broadcasting Corporation, where he was one of the founders of an ethnic program on the radio, Head of the Community Relation Centers, and a senior executive in the Norwegian Government Immigration Department, the Swedish Immigration Board, and the United Nations High Commissioner for Refugees. For one person to have so many appointments from a variety of public institutions is a great sign of professional acclaim. His expertise is clearly recognized at the global level. By working for these formal state institutions, he helped tackle the enormous task of incorporating immigrants and refugees into the mainstream. The impact of these contributions has been impressive. As his work demonstrates, he has attained extensive, international recognition and acclaim. The following is a brief detail of his services for these institutions.

The First Intercultural Program on the Radio for Minorities

Dr. Ghani's acclaim first derived from his work as a radio journalist in Oslo in the mid 1970s. He was the first Asian appointed by the Norwegian Ministry of Labor and Cultural Affairs to produce radio programs for the South Asian community in Norway. Thus, Dr. Ghani was one of the founders of ethnic radio programs sponsored by the Norwegian government. It was a unique task because, up until that time, Norwegian society was quite homogeneous, with little experience with integrating immigrants. The purpose of these programs was to promote good community relations and encouraged immigrants' integration into Norwegian society. Integration is a social phenomenon of how individuals actively become part of the host society and how the host society invites them to become members. This issue is of extreme importance because, when immigrants are not integrated into or made a part of a society, social discord ensues. This social discord often results in racism and discrimination, as well other problems such as unemployment and social injustice. Dr. Ghani encouraged immigrants to learn the host country's language and get education and other professional skills, believing that ignorance of these facts will not only lead to the unsuccessful integration of ethnic minorities but also encourage racism and discrimination to flourish. It is a testament to Dr. Ghani's extraordinary expertise and leadership that he has been chosen to establish, develop, and run radio programs for immigrant communities, which, in turn, promote good community relations and encourage minorities to incorporate into host societies through different cultural, social, and academic programs. These programs were a great success, and subsequently programs in other languages began. Thus, Dr. Ghani was one of the pioneers of ethnic programs in Norway. Acknowledging his services to the community, the Norwegian national daily newspaper, *Aftenposten,* wrote, "This service is responsible for promoting good community relations. Navid Ghani reported news from his home country and Norway in addition to giving advice to immigrants on Norwegian culture and values. Navid Ghani has always promoted the struggle, integration and success of immigrants through these programs" *(Aftenposten,* May 8, 1981).

Establishment of Community Relation Centers

Throughout the 1970s and 1980s, Dr. Ghani was involved in the Asian–Norwegian community, working for racial equality, justice, and promoting harmonious relations within mainstream society. He distinguished himself within his own ethnic group while exemplifying the values of mainstream society. He found many stereotypes and little accurate information on immigrants in schools, libraries, and society in general: the expression *community relations* therefore covers the totality of relations between the native population and ethnic groups of immigrant origin. This approach was necessary because it was clear immigrants would one day return to their countries of origin, which has become a myth because the majority of immigrants end up settling down permanently in their host country. Dr. Ghani believes immigrants are valuable and necessary partners in developing multicultural societies. He emphasizes that immigrants should not be considered a separate group but rather an integral part of society. Public authorities, therefore, have a crucial part to play in developing community relations.

Working for a public institution such as the Norwegian Broadcasting Corporation was the first step in this direction. It provided him the motivation to promote better community relations and future vision for public service. This was a unique task because, up until 20 years ago, Norwegian society was quite homogeneous, with little experience with immigrants from non-European countries and assimilating them into Norwegian society. At the grass roots level, Dr. Ghani creatively devised a series of measures to help the Norwegian government integrate immigrants and for immigrants to understand how the government could provide them services. Perhaps one of his greatest contributions was the establishment of an intercommunal information center to provide the tools necessary for integrating immigrants into the local community by celebrating diversity and promoting an understanding of each other's cultural norms and values.

This community center serves as an "advocate" for groups that are often deprived of information, unfamiliar with the ins and outs of the Norwegian administrative machinery, and hampered by language barriers and prejudices. In doing so, he has helped many immigrants each year. Such services, drawing upon the need for immigrants to have adequate language translation and awareness of their rights and obligations in their own language, was the first of its kind in Oslo, and it was well received by community leaders and the public sector. Subsequently, different community centers have been established throughout Norway, with Dr. Ghani playing a major advisory and consultancy role. He traveled around the country to lecture on the importance of integration and community relations and

184

strongly believed the successful integration of minorities was essential for harmonious and peaceful societies. The local newspaper, *Nationen,* described his overall contributions to Norwegian society as a "Magnificent achievement" that helped immigrants and refugees integrate into Norwegian society (*Nationen, April 4, 1986*).

Thus, Dr. Ghani quickly became an expert in implementing services at the community level, such as radio services for the community, communal and inter-communal information and interpreter centers, and preventative lectures on integration, diversity, and tolerance around the country. Each of these initiatives has made a significant contribution in chipping away the cultural and political barriers felt by immigrants. At these positions, Dr. Ghani produced an important report titled, "Community Information Services in Norway," which was widely distributed in Norway and other Nordic countries.

The Norwegian Immigration Department

His next step was working with the Norwegian government. In recognition of his expertise and diverse background, he was hired by the Norwegian Immigration Department to various positions such as senior executive officer, head of division, and senior advisor in a short span of time. He also worked as an acting deputy director on many occasions and serves the department with vigor and hard work. He was the first Pakistani-born Norwegian to hold these positions in the Norwegian Immigration Department, which was a rare phenomenon at that time. On his appointment, the Norwegian national daily newspaper, *Aftenposten* wrote, "Asians are the fastest growing group in Norway. It is most appropriate that a distinguished Asian-Norwegian is named to these very important positions" (*Aftenposten,* April 1987).

Dr. Ghani has been actively engaged in opposing racism and other form of antidemocratic social forces such as anti-Islam and anti-Semitism and other forms of hate. He believes there should be no place in our democratic societies for religious hatred, no matter which religion people belong to. He advocated multicultural understanding and tolerance by saying, "the existence of cultural diversity should be a source of pride, not hostility. The diversity creates a responsibility to reduce the institutionalized and non-institutionalized aspects of racism" (*Aftenposten,* April 1987). In one of his other interviews, he said, "Our differences are our dignity. Respect is learning how to live with other differences" (*Aftenposten,* November 20, 1986).

Working for the Norwegian government, Dr. Ghani has been employed in critical and essential responsibilities. In his leadership role, he was involved in designing the governments' contingency plan to receive refugees from former Soviet bloc countries. Dr. Ghani reviewed applications and allocated funds for over $1.25 million in grants for communal and regional authorities to help them with an eventual refugee crisis. Based on the success of providing secure housing for the refugees, Dr. Ghani was requested on various occasions to speak about Norway's refugee plan. Government officials from the United Kingdom, Sweden, Finland, Canada, and the European Union Commission in Strasbourg, France, invited Dr. Ghani to lecture on Norway's successes in managing immigration and refugee issues.

Member of a Prestigious Norwegian Housing Committee

Over the years, many local and national newspapers have recognized his public and community services. In January 1985, on the recommendation of the Norwegian Prime Minister Gro Harlem Brundtland, Dr. Ghani was appointed as a member of the Public Housing Committee for immigrants and refugees, a very prestigious and influential position requiring a royal decree from the king, and an official pronouncement in the Council of State. On his appointment, the Norwegian national newspaper, *Aftenposten* highlighted his achievement and wrote, "Navid Ghani became the first Asian immigrant ever elected to such a prestigious position, a right position for a right man" *(Aftenposten,* November 21, 1986). Dr. Ghani was distinguished with this honor because of his community-level services. After receiving confirmation of the appointment, Dr. Ghani said he was "humbled" to receive the honor because he believed there were "many others who deserved it" more than him.

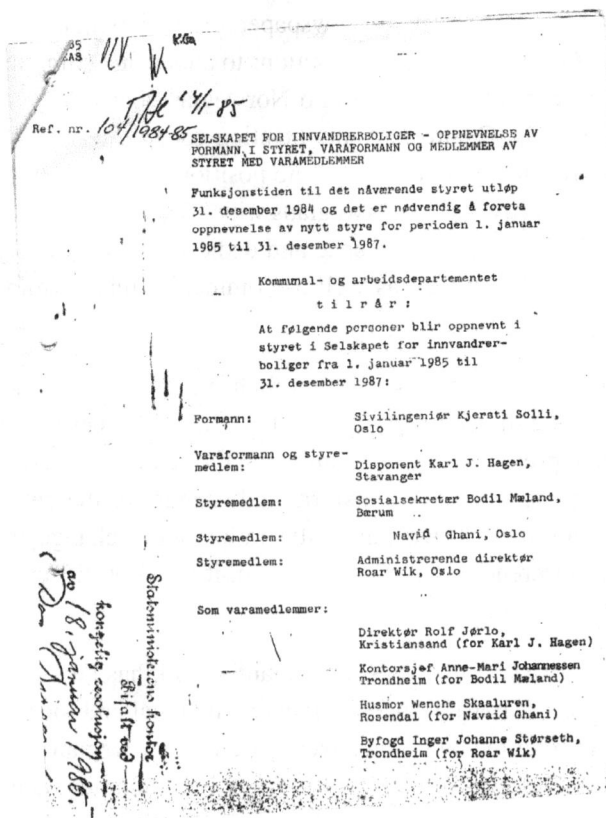

Image 3: The Royal Decree appointing the author as a member of the Public Housing Committee
Source: Author

The purpose of this prestigious public housing committee was to provide affordable housing for immigrants and refugees, as well as for Norwegians in need of economic assistance. In his role, Dr. Ghani was able to provide a great deal of funding for immigrants in the form of public loans to buy homes as well as to rehabilitate the antiquated housing structures in which immigrants often lived. He gained national exposure as a first ever-Asian member of this prestigious committee. All major newspapers in Norway covered this appointment on their front pages and its editorials. On the 10th anniversary of the Public Housing Committee, the top political leadership, which included the prime minister, speaker of the parliament, and the mayor of Oslo, and other prominent local and business leaders were invited to celebrate the occasion. The Norwegian prime minister on the occasion called Dr. Ghani a "man of diverse ability and a bridge builder."

Norway's second largest daily newspaper, *Arbeiderbladet,* covering the story, portrayed Dr. Ghani's life and contributions to public and community service as an example of successful integration into Norwegian society *(Arbeiderbladet,* November 26, 1986). Dr. Ghani held this position for two terms (1985–1992), which is an impressive distinction. This public position gave him the opportunity to help minorities and needy native Norwegians with grants and cheap loans to buy affordable homes. Because of his influence and dedication, the housing condition for ethnic minorities and refugees, as well as community relationship, improved dramatically.

Dr. Ghani always downplayed racial prejudice in Norway. Although he did not deny there had been discrimination against Asians and other people of color. He always stated that prejudice and discrimination thrive in all societies; however, in democracies, people can always transform and change for the better. He cited his own success as an Asian-Norwegian as illustration of that change and says that, in spite of cultural differences and discrimination, it was not difficult to achieve success in Norwegian society.

With such impressive accolades, Dr. Ghani's work has been the subject of much published material. For instance, Norwegian national and local newspapers on various occasions reported on his achievements. The Norwegian prime minister on several occasions appreciated his work for the community and society in general. Dr. Ghani has been the focus of articles in mainstream newspapers such as *Agderposten, Norske Argus, Nationen, Romerikeposten, Arbeiderbladet, and VG.*

Moving to Sweden

Next, to his great credit, Dr. Ghani was awarded a Nordic Fellowship and grant (Nordic Civil Servant Exchange Grant) by the Swedish government, given only to the most outstanding person from across the Nordic countries. This prestigious Fellowship invited him to participate in research and policy analysis of immigration issues at the Swedish Immigration Services, the government agency in charge of immigrant affairs in Sweden. As part of the fellowship, the Swedish government requested a detailed report, examining the condition of immigrants throughout the country. As a Nordic fellow, he moved to Sweden in the early 1990s and traveled extensively in the country and prepared a report aimed at offering policy reform recommendations such as authorizing refugees to work with permits before granting them resident status (an important step decreasing dependence on the state), and adopting standardized interpreter services (essential to educating immigrants and refugees about their rights and obligations in their new country. This report titled, "Nordic Civil Servant Exchange Program" was presented to the government of Norway, Sweden, and the United Nations High Commissioner for Refugees.

WORKING FOR THE UNITED NATIONS

Moving to Switzerland, Iran, and Afghanistan

In the early 1990s, Dr. Ghani became a representative for the United Nations High Commissioner for Refugees and moved to Geneva, Switzerland, for security training. He later moved to Iran, where he assisted the Iranian government with the repatriation of Afghan refugees to their homeland in Afghanistan. Dr. Ghani's role in this process was critical and essential. On repeated occasions, he personally met with military leaders and government officials of Iran, Afghanistan, and Pakistan to devise a repatriation plan for Afghan refugees. Under the repatriation process, Dr. Ghani aided the resettlement of 500,000 refugees back to their homeland. At this time, Iran was suffering greatly, with an estimated two to three million refugees fleeing the Soviet invasion of Afghanistan. The refugees posed enormous socio, economic, and political problems in Iran because they had no legal status in the country and lacked legal protections, a right to earn money, or a right to housing. Similarly, the millions of refugees suffered because they could not return home to Afghanistan. They did not return home because they feared the journey home would be dangerous because warlords, armies, and drug dealers controlled portions of the countryside. Likewise, they had no guarantee they would be welcomed in their homeland by the armies and warlords.

Image 4: *The author (left) at the United Nations conference in Iran*
Source: *Author*

Working with government officials from several countries, including military leaders in Afghanistan, warlords, government officials from Iran and Pakistan, and the United Nations, Dr. Ghani's efforts resulted in the multination-sponsored repatriation program. He was also among the first group of foreigners to travel to the "front line" in the field where the refugees were resettled. This was a remarkable step because the refugees were thousands of miles away from the administrative capitals of Tehran and Kabul. To determine what was needed for repatriation, Dr. Ghani conducted an exhaustive interview and social condition analysis of thousands of refugees scattered in different camps in Iran. This was essential for establishing trust between the stakeholders and convincing them about supportive measures regarding the need to implement a repatriation program for Afghani refugees. Dr. Ghani's participation in this momentous project included the following achievements: securing a safe passage for hundreds of thousands of families in a region plagued by drug dealers, warlords, and soldiers from different nations; establishing a UN refugee outpost in Mashhad, Iran (close to the border of Iran and Afghanistan); implementing a refugee support repatriation program composed of tents, blankets, food, and funds for each refugee who agreed to return to Afghanistan; organizing the first international conference on refugee issues in Tehran in support of the repatriation efforts; establishing the professional support for and implementing refugee travel assistance plans with the Red Cross and NGOs in Iran and Afghanistan; recommending policies to the Iranian government regarding repatriation initiatives; and, perhaps most significantly, bringing together Iran, Afghan, and Pakistani leaders to come to an agreement on how repatriation would be implemented. Ultimately, the program successfully began the repatriation process and proved to be the first successful attempt of its kind in the region. It was a significant achievement for the United Nations and helped resolve enormous tensions between governments involved.

Image 5: with the security staff

Image 6: woman colleague wearing a chador to cover her hair and body

Source: Author

Although the region has seen enormous changes since then, in the mid-1990s, the Afghani refugee problem was one of the international community's most difficult challenges. The problem had existed since 1979, and it greatly hindered economic growth in Iran and inhibited peace in Afghanistan—and overall created instability in the region. The program's success reflects Dr. Ghani's expertise in immigration and refugee issues. Also his role as a senior representative for the UN was undoubtedly critical and essential. Most importantly, because the program was the first to repatriate these refugees, his expertise resulted in an enormous contribution for the UN and the region. Dr. Ghani worked for a couple of years for the United Nations before returning back to Norway, where his wife was pregnant with their second child, and he wanted to be with her. Therefore, he did not renew his contract with the United Nations, a decision he still very much regrets.

Image 7: *Lunch with colleagues from the United Nations*
Source: *Author*

At the end of his mission, Dr. Ghani wrote a comprehensive report on, "Afghan Refugees in Iran," with recommendations. He also proposed a tripartite regional conference between Iran, Pakistan, and Afghanistan to provide the motivational grounds for the eventual return of Afghan refugees to their homeland.

Image 8: *Meeting with Pakistani official*   ***Image 9:*** *With Danish ambassador*
Source: *Author*

His superiors in the United Nations appreciated his report and recommendations. Louis Barbeau, the head of the UN Mission in Iran, considered this report "very useful" for the United Nations' effort in Iran and elsewhere to resettle refugees in their home country.

Image 10: a get-together with Head of the United Nations mission, Louis Barbeau (far right)
Source: *Author*

Image 11: author with his wife
Source: *Author*

MOVING TO THE UNITED STATES

Research, publications, and presentations

Dr. Ghani has been an extraordinary and significant contributor in the field of immigration and ethnic and race relations since he moved to the United States in 1996 for higher studies. As an academic and scholar, his notoriety is extremely well known. He has served as a college and university professor, and his research studies are extensively published in leading scholarly forums. It is important to note that Dr. Ghani's scholarly acclaim began after he had a noteworthy career in public service, working with immigration and community relations issues, specifically, his appointment with the United Nations, the Norwegian Directorate of Immigration, Norwegian Broadcasting Cooperation, and the Swedish Immigration Board. From these leading positions, Dr. Ghani gained an invaluable knowledge base in regard to dealing with the problems host nations face when they receive millions of immigrants and refugees. The crux of his work in the UN, Norway, and Sweden has been problem-solving and developing new public policies. With this solution-based and policy-making perspective, Dr. Ghani's sociology research has been ground-breaking. This work began with his research at the Stony Brook University at Stony Brook, New York, where he received his master's degree (1999) and a PhD (2003) in research-oriented studies. An important element of his research is taking both a theoretical and policy-based approach to examining immigration issues. In doing so, he provides recommendations for how local, state, and national governments can improve issues such as the prevalence of racism or the objective of immigrant integration; his research has greatly improved how the discipline creates new solutions to long-term problems. Thus, his research and recommendations, which were implemented by the United Nations, Iran, Afghanistan, Sweden, and Norway, provided vital and pioneering policies on how to house millions of refugees from the Soviet invasion of Afghanistan and the civil wars in the former Yugoslavia. Recent events in the Middle East, Central Africa, Central Asia, South America, and, most recently, in Europe (i.e., Ukraine) show that refugees are increasing in number throughout the world. Dr. Ghani's expertise and contributions in this field are well-established and documented.

His scholarly contributions in the United States include his repeated participation in professional conferences in the United States, where he lectured on the topic of immigration, community relations, and related issues, educating Americans about the most important debates in the ethnic literature today. These conferences include (but are not limited to) the World Congress on Refugee Issues in Iran, Nordic Linguistic Convention in Finland; the International Conferences on

Interpreting and Health Services in Toronto; the Biannual Conference on the Nordic Convention in Sweden and Finland (twice); Muslim Migrants in the United States: The Interplay of Ethnic Identity and Ethnic Retention, Las Vegas; Integration and Changing Patterns of Ethnic Affiliation among Pakistani Muslim College Students in New York; Integration through Equal Opportunity, Honolulu; Strangers in a Strange Land: Immigration Policy in the Bush Era, panel discussion at Hofstra University, Long Island, New York; the Conference on Diversity in Research and Society in New York; and the American Sociologist Association's Conferences in Washington, DC, and Chicago. In addition, he was a visiting speaker at the University of Oslo and at Stockholm University in Sweden, where he spoke about immigration and immigrant-related issues.

Dr. Ghani has published numerous abstracts in the highly acclaimed *American Sociological Abstracts*, the official publication of the American Sociological Association.

The significant lessons gleaned from Dr. Ghani's vast scholarly and research experiences in the field of ethnic and race relations have garnered him sustained international and national acclaim for his superior research activities. An important element of his research combining both a theoretical and policy-based approach to examining immigration and minority-related issues. By posing important theoretical issues such as the prevalence of the racism or the objective of better community relations, his research greatly improves how the discipline creates new solutions to long-term problems. Likewise, his research identifies methods for governments to assess the economic impact, in terms of public costs and benefits, of foreign-born labor. Importantly, Dr. Ghani's research involves intense, exhaustive, and statistics-based economic analysis. This is an enormous contribution for policy makers, who consistently ask how programs and objectives weigh on public budgets and the private economy. Additionally, his research provides a comparative approach, by looking at how different ethnic groups, age groups, geographic areas, and countries respond to the challenges of host nations in the context of community relations and integration of ethnic minorities in the mainstream population.

His published work on Islamophobia, racism, hate groups, immigration, diversity and related issues is widely read by many scholars, students, and policy makers, and it has received very favorable comments. Thus, his work has the potential to make a significant impact on American society and societies throughout the world, practicing in the field of immigration and race relations.

Hence, all these activities have greatly contributed to the practical knowledge in the field and should be considered of national interest.

Dr. Ghani also served as a judge of the work of others in the research and public administration fields. He served as a reviewer for several journals—for example, *Journal of American Sociological Review, Journal of Critical Sociology,* and *Journal of Equal Opportunity,* to name a few. A reviewer decides whether a submission's research is empirically sound, original to the field, theoretically accurate, and important to the field. A reviewer therefore must be an expert researcher, completely versed in the field's latest developments. Central to this function is Dr. Ghani evaluating, judging, and critiquing the work of other scholars. To review for a journal is a great sign of scholarly pride. His work in this regard illustrates a significant contribution to scholarship because these journals are the most prestigious publications in the field and admired across the globe.

Dr. Ghani's main work and recent publications in American and international academic and scholarly journals include *Islamophobia in the United States* (2022); *the Role of Media and Islamophobia in the United States* (2021); *the Rise of Islamophobia in the United States: Patterns, Perpetrators, and Responses* (2018); *Muslim Migrants in the United States: The Interplay of Ethnic Identity and Ethnic Retention* (2016); *Minimum Wage and Its Impact on Business* (2016); *Integration and Development of Ethnic Identity: Second Generation Muslim Americans in Contemporary New York* (2015); *Cultural Movements: Global Perspective* (2015); *Cultural Movements and Their Impact on Business and Marketing* (2014); *Diversity, Racism, and Xenophobia: Global Implications* (2009); *Integration and the Formation of Ethnic Identity among South Asian Immigrants in Norway* (2008); *Economic Impact of Immigration* (2008); *Current and Future Perspectives on Migration* (2005); *Integration through Equal Opportunity in a Scandinavian Welfare State (2003); Welfare and Public Benefits by Immigrants in the United States* (2001).

Forthcoming

Racism in the 21st Century

Email address: nghani1000@yahoo.com